D0950192

Praise for
WHEN GOD SPEAKS

With clarity and precision, Chuck Pierce has brought forth a
sparkling gem full of revelatory truth in the pages of *When God Speaks*.
This book is a great addition to the arsenal of prophetic materials
that will enable the current move of God to progressively keep on
marching forward. *When God Speaks* is one of the clearest exposés
I have ever read on hearing God's voice.

JAMES W. GOLL
President, Encounters Network
Author, *The Seer*, *The Lost of Intercession* and *Wasted on Jesus*

In the critical times we are living in today, it is more imperative than
ever for believers to learn to discern the Voice of the Lord. In *When God Speaks*,
Chuck Pierce demystifies the experience of God communicating to
His people and helps us to grasp the unique and varied ways God
speaks. This is a dynamic equipping tool that should be in the
spiritual arsenal of every believer.

JANE HAMON
Author, *Dreams and Visions*

The practice of two-way prayer is much more common than it
used to be. This makes it extremely important for us to be able to
clearly recognize God's voice whenever He wants to speak to us.
There is no better guidebook to make this happen than Chuck Pierce
and Rebecca Sytsema's *When God Speaks*!

C. PETER WAGNER
Chancellor, Wagner Leadership Institute

WHEN
GOD
SPEAKS

Chuck D. Pierce
Rebecca Wagner Sytsema

Regal

From Gospel Light
Ventura, California, U.S.A.

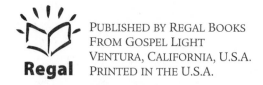

PUBLISHED BY REGAL BOOKS
FROM GOSPEL LIGHT
VENTURA, CALIFORNIA, U.S.A.
PRINTED IN THE U.S.A.

Regal Books is a ministry of Gospel Light, a Christian publisher dedicated to serving the local church. We believe God's vision for Gospel Light is to provide church leaders with biblical, user-friendly materials that will help them evangelize, disciple and minister to children, youth and families.

It is our prayer that this Regal book will help you discover biblical truth for your own life and help you meet the needs of others. May God richly bless you.

For a free catalog of resources from Regal Books/Gospel Light, please call your Christian supplier or contact us at 1-800-4-GOSPEL *or* www.regalbooks.com.

All Scripture quotations, unless otherwise indicated, are taken from the *New King James Version*. Copyright © 1979, 1980, 1982 by Thomas Nelson, Inc. Used by permission. All rights reserved.

Other versions used are
AMP–Scripture taken from THE AMPLIFIED BIBLE, Old Testament copyright © 1965, 1987 by the Zondervan Corporation. The Amplified New Testament copyright © 1958, 1987 by The Lockman Foundation. Used by permission.
KJV–*King James Version*. Authorized King James Version.
NIV–Scripture taken from the *Holy Bible, New International Version*®. Copyright © 1973, 1978, 1984 by International Bible Society. Used by permission of Zondervan Publishing House. All rights reserved.
NLT–Scripture quotations marked *(NLT)* are taken from the *Holy Bible*, New Living Translation, copyright © 1996. Used by permission of Tyndale House Publishers, Inc., Wheaton, Illinois 60189. All rights reserved.

Originally published by Wagner Publications in 2003.
Regal Books edition published in July 2005.

© 2005 Chuck D. Pierce and Rebecca Wagner Sytsema
All rights reserved.

Library of Congress Cataloging-in-Publication Data
Pierce, Chuck D., 1953-
    When God speaks / Chuck D. Pierce, Rebecca Wagner Sytsema.
        p. cm.
    Includes bibliographical references and index.
    ISBN 0-8307-3707-3 (trade pbk.)
    1. Prophecy–Christianity. I. Sytsema, Rebecca Wagner. II. Title.
    BR115.P8P54 2005
    234'.13–dc22   2005007297

1   2   3   4   5   6   7   8   9   10   /   10   09   08   07   06   05

Rights for publishing this book in other languages are contracted by Gospel Light Worldwide, the international nonprofit ministry of Gospel Light. Gospel Light Worldwide also provides publishing and technical assistance to international publishers dedicated to producing Sunday School and Vacation Bible School curricula and books in the languages of the world. For additional information, visit www.gospellightworldwide.org; write to Gospel Light Worldwide, P.O. Box 3875, Ventura, CA 93006; or send an e-mail to info@gospellightworldwide.org.

CONTENTS

PREFACE

Hearing the voice of God is not as difficult as some might think. I have found that many of God's people are hearing Him, but they have not perceived that it is His voice. To perceive means to take hold of, feel, comprehend, grasp mentally, recognize, observe or become aware of something by discerning. We must learn to perceive God's voice, which will help us understand His will for our lives. Acting on what we have discerned as His voice, until it becomes a reality, is the key to a successful Christian life.

To commune with a holy God—you talk to Him and He to you—is the highest privilege we have on Earth. My own life has become one of hearing the Lord's voice, not just for myself but for others as well. My greatest desire is for people to hear God's voice, embrace His word and fulfill the destiny God has for them.

I pray that this book will give you the principles of hearing God through prophecy and revelation, show you how to test and evaluate the prophetic word, and help you to know what to do with what God has spoken to you. As you read this book, may you recognize the voice that gives you life and life abundantly!

Chuck D. Pierce
Denton, Texas

CHAPTER ONE

HEAR HIM!

*Then God said, "Let Us make man in Our image, according to Our likeness;
let them have dominion over the fish of the sea, over the birds of the air, and
over the cattle, over all the earth and over every creeping thing that creeps on
the earth." So God created man in His own image; in the image of God He
created him; male and female He created them. Then God blessed them,
and God said to them, "Be fruitful and multiply; fill the earth and subdue it;
have dominion over the fish of the sea, over the birds of the air, and over
every living thing that moves on the earth."*

G E N E S I S   1 : 2 6 - 2 8

From the beginning of creation, humanity was created to commune with God. Because God created us with a body, soul and spirit, we were given a different value from the rest of creation. We were made as spiritual beings. Our human spirit allows us to exercise intelligence, perception and determination, and to make moral choices; and it enables us to exceed above and have dominion over any other creature in the earth realm. This intrinsic worth drives us to know our creator as well as to know the hope of our calling and why we exist.

Because we are set apart in this way, we also carry an accountability and responsibility that the rest of creation does not have. We are expected to be faithful stewards of the talents and abilities that God has given us. The only way we can do this is to seek Him, commune with Him and gain the revelation that will enable us to prosper. When we obey this revelation from Him, we please Him.

WE WERE CREATED TO COMMUNE WITH HIM DAILY

The spirit is the highest function of our being. It is through our spirit that we commune with the spiritual world. When we open our human spirit and allow the Holy Spirit to come and reside within us, we come into a holy union with our Creator. It is through our human spirits that the Holy Spirit gives us the revelation necessary to accomplish His will on the earth. Because this is an ongoing process, we should expect God to commune with us daily as we seek Him. He longs for us to draw near to Him so we can know His heart and greatest desire for our lives.

To seek means to diligently look for and search earnestly until the object of desire is located and found. Psalm 27:4-8 says:

One thing I have desired of the LORD, that will I seek: that I may dwell in the house of the LORD all the days of my life, to behold the beauty of the LORD, and to inquire in His temple. For in the time of trouble He shall hide me in His pavilion; in the secret place of His tabernacle He shall hide me; He shall set me high upon a rock. And now my head shall be lifted up above my enemies all around me; therefore I will offer sacrifices of joy in His tabernacle; I will sing, yes, I will sing praises to the LORD. Hear, O LORD, when I cry with my voice! Have mercy also upon me, and answer me. When You said, "Seek My face," my heart said to You, "Your face, LORD, I will seek."

David was known as a man with a heart after God because he was willing to seek God until he received the Lord's mind and strategy for that hour. That is also why Jesus said, "But seek first the kingdom of God and His righteousness, and all these things shall be added to you" (Matt. 6:33).

Moses gives us a beautiful example of and reason why we should be seeking God on a daily basis. In Exodus 29, we find Moses receiving revelation on the daily offerings two times each day. The day is opened and closed with the gift of worship to and communion with God. Verse 42 says, "This shall be a continual burnt offering throughout your generations at the door of the tabernacle of meeting before the LORD, *where I will meet you to speak with you*" (emphasis added). What a wonderful principle for us! If we will come before God on a daily basis, He will meet us, join with us and speak to us. He will set us apart for service. We will begin to sense His presence. We will have assurance that He is with us. He will take a stand against our enemies. "And they shall know that I am the LORD their God, who brought them up out . . . " (v. 46). We will know that He is the God who will keep us safe, deliver us from evil and lead us into all the promises and destiny He has for our lives.

GOD SPEAKS

I was eight years old when I first became aware that God had a voice and actually spoke to people. My godly grandmother would take me to a little Baptist church in East Texas where we lived. A lady named Mrs. Grimes would do a very peculiar thing. Right in the middle of the preacher's message, Mrs. Grimes would stand up and wave her hands. Being a Baptist church, this was very unusual behavior. Yet the preacher would stop his message and ask her what was happening. Mrs. Grimes would say, "The Lord is speaking to me!" Then the pastor would say, "Tell us what He's saying." And Mrs. Grimes would begin to tell us what she was hearing from the Spirit of God and how it affected the church.

It totally fascinated me that God could really speak to people. When the preacher talked about God, it seemed boring and dry. But when Mrs. Grimes would speak up, it was filled with life and vibrancy. I would look up at my grandmother and say, "If God can speak to that woman, I want Him to speak to me." My grandmother would look down at me—a typically wild eight-year-old boy—and say, "You will have to learn to be quiet and sit still for God to ever say anything to you!"

My Day of Salvation

From that point on, there was no question in my mind that God had a voice. I had heard it through Mrs. Grimes and in the Bible stories taught in Sunday School. Still, I never heard Him speak directly to me—until I was 11 years old. One Sunday during a service, the Spirit of the Lord came to me and clearly said, "This is your day." It was as if I followed His Spirit up to the altar and surrendered my life to Him as best as an 11-year-old child can.

As I studied the Bible later on, it became clear to me that God has a day of salvation for each one of us (see 2 Cor. 6:2). We all come into our day of salvation by hearing God's voice speak into our spirit, which up to that point is dead in trespasses. As we respond to His voice and allow Him to illuminate truth in our darkened spirit, we come into our day of salvation. In fact, none of us have been saved without the voice of God prompting us. We may not have heard an audible voice, but because only God can illuminate the truth of salvation, all who have had a salvation experience and know Jesus as their Lord and Savior have heard God's voice, whether or not they understood it at the time! It is this same voice that quickens the Word of God to us. Therefore, every time we glean truth from Scripture, we hear God at some level.

"I Will Restore"

Even though I had been saved, I had a difficult and often traumatic and abusive childhood. My family had suffered great loss and anguish. Much of my family fell apart during my teen years as a result of the enemy's inroads into my father's life. He then died under tragic circumstances when I was 16. By the time I turned 18, my body had begun to suffer from working, going to college and having a fairly ardent nightlife.

Eventually, I wound up in the hospital suffering from exhaustion and double pneumonia. It was while I was in the hospital that the Lord clearly spoke to me in an audible voice and said, "I will restore all that you have lost." With those words He penetrated every part of my being. Though I had suspected it before, I now *knew* that God had a plan not only to go back and heal the wounds of my past, but also to restore my future.

I had never before seen the concept of restoration in the Bible, but as I read more deeply, I learned that God's voice had the power to restore (see Joel 2:25). My whole life changed from that moment; and since that time, God has healed, delivered and restored me in miraculous ways.[1] God's voice has great power to

God's voice has great power to bring us out of the ruins of our past and set us on the course He has ordained for our lives.

bring us out of the ruins of our past and set us on the course He has ordained for our lives, as I learned on that day many years ago.

YOUR TESTIMONY IS POWERFUL

As you read, this may be a good place for you to stop and think about how the voice of God has manifested in your life. How were you saved? How has God supernaturally affected your life and your circumstances? You might want to write out your testimony. The reason for writing it out is because there is great power in the word of your testimony; it builds faith as nothing else can.

Our testimony is an important function of the human spirit. Think of the Ark of the Covenant. Several items were in the ark, one of which was the testament that God gave to Moses. When we commune with God through the Word, we store His precepts and principles down deep in our hearts, where we have established covenant with God. When we obey these precepts and principles and experience God's faithfulness, we develop a testimony that has great power against our enemy. Once we have an established testimony, we can refute the lies of the devil by saying, "God has spoken this to me. Because I have seen His hand move in the past, I know He will do the same now, for nothing is impossible to Him!"

Revelation 12:10 says, "Then I heard a loud voice saying in heaven, 'Now salvation, and strength, and the kingdom of our God, and the power of His Christ have come, for the accuser of our brethren, who accused them before our God day and night, has been cast down. And they overcame him by the blood of the Lamb and by the word of their testimony.'" The enemy cannot withstand the voice of God coupled with the power of our testimony.

GOD'S VOICE IS CREATIVE

In the account of creation in Genesis, we see that the creative instrument God used again and again was His voice. God *spoke* into chaos and light came into being. He *spoke* again and light divided from darkness, creating day and night. The power of His voice created the heavens and earth, and the abundance of creatures filled the earth and seas.

God's voice is so powerful that it can divide substance. From the power of His voice, substance can be made into a different form. God made the ground from His creative voice, and from that ground He formed human beings. Our very being is, therefore, a product of His creative voice.

JESUS SPEAKS

Jesus was God as man who came to Earth to redeem the human race and to present the full character of God to us. Part of that character was the power of His voice. When Jesus spoke, things happened. His public ministry began in John 2 when He and His mother attended a wedding. When the wedding feast ran short of wine, Jesus' mother told the servants, "Whatever He says to you, do it" (v. 5). It was Jesus' creative voice (the creative voice of God through Jesus as God and man) that changed the water into wine.

Whenever Jesus spoke, He carried great authority. When He raised Lazarus from the dead, Jesus *spoke* to the grave and to the shroud of death surrounding Lazarus and commanded them to loose Lazarus and let him go. Upon Jesus' command, life once again began to flow through Lazarus (see John 11:43). His voice was so powerful that even death and decay were overcome and destroyed.

THE HOLY SPIRIT SPEAKS *TO* AND *THROUGH* US

The Holy Spirit was released to operate in greater measure in the transitional chapter of John 20. Jesus had already been crucified, had died and been raised from the dead, but He had not yet ascended to heaven. Jesus knew that He had to equip His disciples with power to accomplish their role on Earth, because He was now leaving to be with the Father. In John 20:22, we read, "He breathed on them, and said to them, 'Receive the Holy Spirit.'"

As the Holy Spirit was released to them, He began to speak *to* them and *through* them on an ongoing basis. The Holy Spirit spoke many times *to* them, including when He instructed Peter to go to the house of Cornelius (see Acts 10). But prophecy was birthed in a whole new way as the Holy Spirit began to speak *through* them on a consistent basis. In Acts, the account of Stephen records, "and they were not able to resist the wisdom and the Spirit by which he spoke" (Acts 6:10). Here the Holy Spirit spoke *through* Stephen.

THE WORD SPEAKS

In addition to each member of the Trinity having a voice, God has also supplied us with His written Word to speak into our lives. God told Joshua,

> Only be strong and very courageous, that you may observe to do according to all the law which Moses My servant commanded you; do not turn from it to the right hand or to the left, that you may prosper wherever you go. This Book of the Law shall not depart from your mouth, but you shall meditate in it day and night, that you may observe to do according to all that is written in it. For then you will make your way prosperous, and then you will have good success (Josh. 1:7-8).

In the New Testament, we find in John 1:14, "And the Word became flesh and dwelt among us, and we beheld His glory, the glory as of the only begotten of the Father, full of grace and truth." This Scripture describes the unique, loving relationship of the Son with the Father and how we understand that relationship through the Word. By meditating on the Word, we reflect, ponder, contemplate and repeat God's will for our lives. We remove all distractions; it's just God and us interacting. His Word becomes a light to our path. As we order our prayers and communion, His Word orders our feet. His truths and principles guide us. By knowing the Word of God, we know Him and can recognize His voice and how He operates in the earth. The Word is the blueprint of heaven and the blueprint of life. "Today, if you will hear His voice, do not harden your hearts as in the rebellion" (Heb. 3:15).

GOD'S VOICE IN OUR LIVES

Every member of the Trinity operates powerfully through speaking. God's voice commands great authority and continues to be creative today, even in the situations that occur in our lives. Whenever our lives are filled with chaos, as the heavens and earth once were, God's voice can come into our situations and bring order, dividing the light from the darkness.

Furthermore, God speaks to us more often than we may be aware. Consider the fact that throughout the Bible, in both the Old and New Testaments, God spoke to His people frequently. He spoke to the kings, the judges, the prophets, the shepherds and the disciples. He spoke to old and young alike. He spoke to those in powerful positions and to those with no social status. He spoke to the righteous and the sinners. From Genesis to Revelation, God spoke to all kinds of people.

There is absolutely no Scripture in the Bible that even suggests that God stopped speaking when the last word of the Bible was written. Throughout the ages, God has continued to speak to His people. If you have accepted Christ as your Savior and Lord, this includes you! He speaks direction, comfort, insight, correction, exhortation, promises and the like to His people today. "Anyone who is willing to hear should listen to the Spirit and understand what the Spirit is saying" (Rev. 2:7, *NLT*).

Today, because the blood of Jesus has redeemed us, the Holy Spirit is locking us in to the Father's heart. But here again, the Holy Spirit is not only speaking *to* us, He is also speaking *through* us. When God formed us with His creative voice, He made us in His image, according to His likeness, and gave us dominion over all the earth (see Gen. 1:26). Because we were created in His image and have been redeemed by Christ, we have the ability, through the power of the Holy Spirit, *to be the voice of God on the earth*. The Holy Spirit is speaking *through* us to one another, and to a lost and dying world. That is what it means to be an ambassador for Christ, and that is what prophecy is all about.

Note

1. For a more complete account of this story, see Chuck D. Pierce and Rebecca Wagner Sytsema, *Possessing Your Inheritance* (Ventura, CA: Renew Books, 1999.)

CHAPTER TWO

SPEAKING GOD'S WORDS:

PROPHECY IN TODAY'S WORLD

And it shall come to pass in the last days, says God,
that I will pour out of My Spirit on all flesh; your sons and your
daughters shall prophesy, your young men shall see visions,
your old men shall dream dreams.

ACTS 2:17

IS PROPHECY FOR TODAY?

Most Christians in the United States grew up in churches that did not embrace the idea of God speaking to us today. We were taught cessationism, which means that the power gifts of healing, tongues, interpretation of tongues, miracles and the like all ceased to function in the first century. One of the gifts that supposedly stopped functioning was prophecy. What that basically means is that God said all He had to say by A.D. 95 and has been silent ever since.

Those who hold to this line of thinking believe that prophecy passed away when the Scriptures were completed. They base their belief on 1 Corinthians 13:8-9, which says that prophecy, tongues and knowledge will pass away. However, in the following chapter of 1 Corinthians, Paul encourages us to desire prophecy (see 14:1). He did not say that these gifts would be replaced by any others or that they would pass away before the second coming of Christ.

In fact, in Ephesians 4, Paul writes,

And He Himself gave some to be apostles, some prophets, some evangelists, and some pastors and teachers, for the equipping of the saints for the work of ministry, for the edifying of the body of Christ, *till we all come to the unity of the faith and of the knowledge of the Son of God, to a perfect man, to the measure of the stature of the fullness of Christ* (vv. 11-13, emphasis added).

In this passage, we see that these gifts have been given *until* we come to unity and reach the stature of the fullness of Christ. At no time in the history of the Church have we achieved these things. Therefore, based on Paul's own words, these gifts, including prophecy, are still in operation today.

HOW CAN WE KNOW THE WILL OF GOD?

The Bible makes it very clear that God has a purpose and a plan for our lives. Any biblical scholar will agree that this did not end in the first century. But if we have a God that doesn't speak to us, it will be hard to discern what that plan is. Many of us have read books or heard messages on knowing the will of God, which are filled with good principles to follow. Yet, the fact remains that the Bible only gives one real principle to follow in trying to determine God's will for our lives. In the Bible, when someone wanted to know the will of God, they asked Him—and He told them!

Our God constantly pours out new revelation and is continually speaking to His people. He is a God who loves us enough to want to enter into communication with us.

God *does* speak to His people. But if we are so entrenched in a mind-set that says God does *not* speak today, we might as well write it off as imagination. The truth is that the prophetic is not an optional extra in the Christian life or in the Church. Amos 3:7 goes so far as to say, "Surely the Lord GOD does nothing, unless He reveals His secret to His servants the prophets."

Throughout the Bible, God communicated with His people. In 1 Corinthians 12, Paul reminded the Gentiles that they once worshiped mute idols. What a foolish thing to worship something that cannot communicate! Our God, however, is not like the mute idols. Our God constantly pours out new revelation and is continually speaking to His people. He is a God who loves us enough to want to enter into communication with us.

WHAT IS PROPHECY?

The definition of prophecy is simple. Prophecy is speaking the mind and heart of God as revealed by the Holy Spirit. Prophecy is the outflow of the heart and the very nature of God. Revelation 19:10 says that the testimony of Jesus is the spirit of prophecy. Jesus cares about His Church and therefore, has things He wants to communicate to His Church. Those communications come by way of the Holy Spirit. That is prophecy. It is what Jesus is saying to His Church.

The testimony of Jesus, which is prophecy, is not just a corporate promise. Jesus says that His sheep know His voice (see John 10:4). If you are one of His sheep, you have the capability, the capacity and the privilege of hearing the voice of your Shepherd that comes through the Holy Spirit.

UNDERSTANDING THE PROPHETS

Several Hebrew and Greek words can be translated as "prophet" throughout the Bible. To understand how prophecy works today, it is helpful to know the different types of prophets and prophecy taught in God's Word. Let's take a look at some of the various names the Bible uses to describe the prophets and their functions:

1. _Nabi._ This is the general Hebrew word for "prophet." It is linked with the word "reveal," and it means one who proclaims, announces, declares or utters communications, or is a spokesman or a herald. This word also implies a supernatural message that bubbles up or springs forth. *Nabi* is the word used in 1 Samuel 3:20: "And all Israel from Dan to Beersheba knew that Samuel had been established as a prophet of the LORD." It can be either masculine or feminine, and can refer to either a prophet of God or a false prophet who brings forth messages contrary to God's character or will.

In John 7:38, Jesus said, "He that believeth on me, as the scripture hath said, out of his belly shall flow rivers of living water" (*KJV*). Paraphrased, this would mean, "out of your womb, a river of revelation can flow." Proverbs 29:18 says, "Where there is no vision [no redemptive revelation of God], the people perish; but he who keeps the law [of God, which includes that of man]— blessed (happy, fortunate, and enviable) is he" (*AMP*). Therefore, it is very important that our river remains flowing or that we are in the presence of others who have a flowing river so that revelation does not stop and we lose sight of our direction.

2. Roeh. This Hebrew word means "seer." These prophets see the circumstances and gain revelation on how to move past them. An example is found in 1 Samuel 9:9: "Come, let us go to the seer." Perhaps the most misunderstood of the prophetic types, seers are the ones who have visions or visual impressions. These types of prophets can look at something and receive a supernatural message through that image. God asked many of the prophets in Scripture, "What do you see?" The Lord has often used this method of communicating with me.

3. Chozeh. This Hebrew word can be translated as a seer who is akin to a watchman. According to the *New Bible Dictionary*, *chozeh* was most often mentioned in association with service to the reigning king.[1]

4. Shamar. This is another Hebrew word translated as "watchman." In *Watchman Prayer*, Dutch Sheet writes, "The three primary Hebrew words in the Old Testament for watchmen are *natsar, shamar* and *tsaphah.* These words have both a defensive or protective connotation and an offensive or aggressive application, with the defensive aspect being the most prominent in the Scriptures. . . . Combining the definitions of these three words, which are almost used synonymously, their defensive concept essentially means *to guard or protect through watching over or concealing.* While applied to many subjects—crops, people, cities, etc.—the concept is usually *preservation.*"[2]

These prophets watched after God's Word and had tremendous wisdom for walking through life. Here are some examples of watchmen: "Also, I set watchmen over you, saying, 'Listen to the sound of the trumpet!'" (Jer. 6:17); "Son of man, I have made you a watchman for the house of Israel; therefore hear a word from My mouth, and give them warning from Me" (Ezek. 3:17). A watchman sees what is coming and links it to the promise of God, interceding until it is accomplished. In 1 Kings 18, Elijah released the word of the Lord to Ahab, which was that it would not rain for three and a half years. At the end of that time, Elijah went into intercession until he "saw" the cloud that represented God's change of seasons. Elijah was acting as a watchman who prophesied God's will and then interceded to see it accomplished.

5. Nataph. This Hebrew word means to preach, to drop as dew from heaven, or to speak by (heavenly) inspiration. This type of prophesying is generally done from a pulpit or in a public place, or is a prophetic word given in the form of an exhortation. The word "*nataph*" is used in Ezekiel 21:2, Amos 7:16 and Micah 2:6. This word deals with oozing or gradually dripping like a trickle from a faucet. In Joel 3:18, the prophet predicted there would come a time when "the mountains shall drip with new wine." This is also predicted in Amos 9:13 concerning the restoration of the Tabernacle of David. As we get closer to

David's Tabernacle being restored, we will begin to see the heavens open wider and wider and God's people living in revelation. Eventually, we will not be hearing "cookie cutter" messages from the pulpit; but when we gather together corporately, we will hear a clear revelatory sound from heaven being brought into the earth realm. This will cause us to develop a walk in the Spirit that the Church has not known in the past few generations.

6. *Prophetes.* This Greek word signifies one who speaks for another, especially one who speaks for God. These are prophets who "forthtell," which means they speak forth a living message from God for the hour. In this context, the prophet is using interpretive gifts to forthtell the will and counsel of God. This word also signifies one who can "foretell" or give insights into future events. In this context, the prophet is using predictive gifts. This is the kind of prophet mentioned in Matthew 2:5, who had written that the Savior would come out of the city of Bethlehem.

THE KEY TO PROPHECY— THE HOLY SPIRIT!

The Holy Spirit is our key to hearing God. Throughout the Bible, in both the Old and New Testaments, whenever the Holy Spirit came, prophecy flowed. Here are just a few examples:

> Then the Spirit of the LORD will come upon you, and you will prophesy (1 Sam. 10:6).

> The Spirit of God came upon the messengers of Saul, and they also prophesied (1 Sam. 19:20).

> And it happened, when the Spirit rested upon them, that they prophesied (Num. 11:25).

And when Paul had laid hands on them, the Holy Spirit came upon them, and they spoke with tongues and prophesied (Acts 19:6).

The Holy Spirit's ministry through prophecy did not end in the first century! In many accounts of revival throughout the Church's history, when the Holy Spirit came in power, prophecy broke loose. In fact, one of the signs of the Spirit's presence is prophecy. Through the Holy Spirit, God acts, reveals His will, empowers individuals and reveals His personal presence. Prophecy is a key element of this process.

WHY IS PROPHECY IMPORTANT?

Prophecy is important because God tells us it is. It's that simple. Here are three biblical reasons to help us understand God's heart toward this important gift.

1. We are to seek to prophesy. "Pursue love, and desire spiritual gifts, but especially that you may prophesy" (1 Cor. 14:1). In the *King James Version*, verse 39 says that we are to "covet to prophecy." Did you know that prophecy is the only thing in the entire Bible that we are supposed to covet? And what happens when we covet something? We think about it all the time. We desire it. We think about what we could do to get it. That's how we are supposed to seek prophecy.

Revelation 2 and 3 state the words of Jesus to many different churches. Jesus gives different admonishments, different promises and different messages to each of the seven churches listed in those passages. The one thing that does not differ from church to church, however, is Jesus' command: "He who has an ear, let him hear what the Spirit says" (Rev. 2:7). We are to hear what the Spirit is saying. We are to seek prophecy.

2. God warns us not to reject prophecy. "Do not despise prophecies. Test all things; hold fast what is good" (1 Thess. 5:20-21). When Paul wrote to the Thessalonians, they were just starting out and still young in the Lord. When something is in the beginning stages, there is often a lack of maturity and a lack of understanding, which can open the door to flakiness. When flakiness springs up, there is a tendency to say that something (in this case prophecy) is more trouble than it's worth. But Paul said to not shut it down. Don't quench the Spirit. Let it happen, test everything and hold on to what is good.

The Bible also tells us not to despise tongues (see 1 Cor. 14:39). The relationship between prophecy and tongues is often misunderstood. Simply put, when a tongue is interpreted, it becomes prophecy.

3. Prophecy releases the life and power of God. As we saw in chapter 1, the word of God has creative power. When Ezekiel saw the dry, dead bones, the Lord told him to prophesy to them:

> So I prophesied as I was commanded; and as I prophesied, there was a noise, and suddenly a rattling; and the bones came together, bone to bone. Indeed, as I looked, the sinews and the flesh came upon them, and the skin covered them over; but there was no breath in them. Also He said to me, "Prophesy to the breath, prophesy, son of man, and say to the breath, 'Thus says the Lord GOD: "Come from the four winds, O breath, and breathe on these slain, that they may live.""" So I prophesied as He commanded me, and breath came into them, and they lived, and stood upon their feet, an exceedingly great army (37:7-10).

When the prophetic word of God goes forth, it doesn't just enlighten you or give you information—it releases life and power. Prophecy changes situations!

UNDERSTANDING THE
GIFT OF PROPHECY

The Holy Spirit equips us to accomplish God's purposes on Earth. This is what 1 Corinthians 12–14 is about. All too often these chapters are separated from one another in the teaching we receive. But the fact is that they were written together and they flow together to help give us an understanding of spiritual gifts and how those gifts are to operate in the Body of Christ. Look at this passage as a whole, in light of the gift of prophecy.

The Body of Christ works in just that way—it is a body, each part having a function and purpose that assists the whole in operating correctly (see 1 Cor. 12:12-26). There are, however, certain gifts to be desired in the Body, one of which is prophecy (see vv. 28-31). From that point, Paul immediately goes into a discourse on the evidences and importance of love. He goes so far as to say, "And though I have the gift of prophecy . . . but have not love, I am nothing" (1 Cor. 13:2).

Paul moves on to say, "Pursue love, and desire spiritual gifts, but especially that you may prophesy" (1 Cor. 14:1). Godly prophecy cannot be separated from love. In fact, true prophecy flows from a heart of love, even if the word is one of correction. The basis for understanding the gift of prophecy is, therefore, understanding issues of love.

FIVE DYNAMIC FUNCTIONS
OF PROPHECY

Having laid out a basic understanding of prophecy, let's now take a look at the various functions of prophecy, based on 1 Corinthians 14. Here is a list of five different purposes for prophecy and what they are meant to accomplish.

1. Comfort. To comfort means to soothe, reassure, bring cheer, bring a feeling of relief from pain or anxiety, lessen one's grief or distress and give strength and hope by means of kindness and thoughtful attention.

> [God is] the Father of mercies and God of all comfort, who comforts us in all our tribulation, that we may be able to comfort those who are in any trouble, with the comfort with which we ourselves are comforted by God. For as the sufferings of Christ abound in us, so our consolation also abounds through Christ (2 Cor. 1:3-5).

God longs to comfort His hurting children. He longs to speak to them in a way that produces strength and hope. This is one of the very basic functions of prophecy that all believers should both receive and deliver to others. A prophetic word of comfort, spoken at the right moment, can break the back of discouragement, hopelessness and anguish!

2. Edification. To edify means to instruct, benefit, uplift, enlighten or build up. First Corinthians 14 is filled with correlations between prophecy and edification, the building up of Christian character. A prophetic word, therefore, may contain elements of teaching, or it may bring new revelation to our minds and spirits. The word may bring specific instruction or a sense of strengthening a place in our lives that has been in desolation or ruins. All of these types of edification can be received from a prophetic word. First Corinthians 8:1 says, "love edifies." Because love is the basis for prophecy, all true prophecies, therefore, have an element of edification.

3. Exhortation. To exhort is to urge, advise, caution, admonish, recommend or warn. A prophetic word that exhorts can therefore either build up or tear down. Exhortation may be difficult to receive. It may not be the word of comfort we hoped for. Even so, words of exhortation are vital in that they bring forth the ultimate purpose of God. Even a difficult word of exhortation that is delivered in the right spirit can leave us feeling a sense of relief and freedom. Prophecy should not leave us with a sense of confusion or condemnation, but rather with a sense of direction and a way of escape from bondage.

4. Redemption. One of the most basic and beautiful functions of prophecy is seeing redemption at work in lives. God's heart, revealed throughout the Bible, is to redeem us from the power of sin and death. Since prophecy is speaking forth the mind of God under the inspiration of the Holy Spirit, the logical conclusion is that prophecy should be redemptive.

Several years ago, a young man named Jon received just such a word from my good friend Cindy Jacobs. Jon was a good husband and father, who was responsible and provided well for his family. He attended church every Sunday and tried his best to follow God. Yet Jon was a closet alcoholic. He was a functional alcoholic, which means that even when he was drunk, few around him knew it. Because he could handle liquor well, he was able to keep secret the fact that he could barely make it through a day without drinking. In addition, he was addicted to chewing tobacco. Yet he knew these things were wrong and had sought God for healing.

During this time in his life, he attended a weekend retreat taught by Cindy. One night, Jon sat quietly in the back while Cindy began giving personal words of prophecy. He felt that God would have nothing to say to him. To his amazement, Cindy pointed to him and called him forward. As he walked toward Cindy, Jon felt sure he was in trouble—as though God was going to publicly rebuke him. But as Cindy began to deliver the prophecy, he could barely believe the words! She told of how the Lord had given Jon the heart of a pastor and how He was going to use Jon in days ahead to see mighty things happen for the kingdom of God!

Jon was stunned. There was no word of rebuke. His secret life was not uncovered. Cindy had prophesied to him about his destiny rather than his addictions. The words were so powerful that Jon was completely delivered that very night from alcoholism and addiction to tobacco. Today, Jon is a governing elder in his church, a cell group leader, a leader of an effective deliverance ministry, and an active member in implementing city-taking strategies in the city in which he lives. Jon will tell you that the turning point in his life was the night when God showed him his redemptive purpose rather than condemning him for his shortcomings. That is redemptive prophecy in action!

5. Direction. As we see throughout the Bible, prophets bring direction to God's people. I have known my coauthor, Rebecca Wagner Sytsema, for many years. In the early '90s, we both served on Cindy Jacobs's staff at Generals of Intercession. During that time, Rebecca went through a two-year period of intensive healing in her life over many issues. I knew that the healing process had brought her to a place where she was ready for marriage. In early 1994, we were preparing to go to a conference in California. One day I looked at her and said, "You need to be at that conference. God has your husband waiting there!"

My words confirmed a feeling that she had been having for about a week, but she had not made her hotel reservations. I immediately picked up the phone and called the hotel where the rest of us were staying. I was told there were no rooms left. I simply told the receptionist that, first, Rebecca's father, Peter Wagner, was in charge of the conference, and, second, her husband would be waiting for her there. The woman on the phone checked again and found one room left. It was at that conference that Rebecca met Jack Sytsema, God's perfect match for her. Two years later, I had the privilege of performing their wedding.

This is a case in which God gave a clear word of direction and then made a way to see His prophesied will come to pass.

THE PROCESS OF PROPHECY

Besides the functions of prophecy, it is important to understand the process of prophecy—that is, how it works in our lives on an ongoing basis. Here are three important elements of the process of prophecy in our lives.

1. Prophecy is progressive. "For we know in part and we prophesy in part" (1 Cor. 13:9). No personal or corporate word of prophecy is complete in and of itself. In his excellent book *Developing Your Prophetic Gifting*, Graham Cooke says,

> God only reveals what we need to know in order to do his will in that particular time and place. The things that he does not wish us to know, he keeps secret from the one prophesying. Elisha said, "The LORD has hidden it from me" (2 Kings 4:27). In other words, "I don't know."[3]

God may give us a little bit here and a little bit there. In retrospect, we may wonder why God didn't tell us this or that, or why He did tell us some seemingly unimportant detail. God always knows what He is doing when He reveals His heart to us through prophecy. That is something that we must simply trust. We must bear in mind, however, that we do not know all that we may encounter or how the prophecies may be fulfilled. Prophecy may point out a path, but we must follow the Lord daily and trust in Him as we move forward.

2. Prophecy evolves. As we follow the Lord in obedience, He will give us our next piece. He will not tell us what He wants us to do three steps down the road. He gives it to us step-by-step. Such was the case with Abraham. God gave him pieces here and there. Each time Abraham obeyed, God would speak to him again until He brought him into the fullness of what He wanted him to do. God confirmed, expanded, gave new insights and moved Abraham on to his next place.

This is the way of prophecy. Each prophetic word is incomplete, yet as we faithfully obey God, we receive new pieces of the puzzle. Prophecies build on earlier prophecies to bring confirmation and fresh understanding.

3. Prophecy is provisional. The key to the process of prophecy is obedience. God will not usurp our wills and force us to follow His will. Mary, for instance, could have said no to the prophetic pronouncement that she would become pregnant. Instead, she responded by saying, "Behold the maidservant of the Lord! Let it be to me according to your word" (Luke 1:38). Had she said no, the Holy Spirit would never have forced her to become pregnant! Although she did not completely understand how this would happen, nor did she probably grasp the magnitude of that for which she had been chosen, she knew, nevertheless, that through the prophetic word God had revealed His destiny for her life. Through her choice of obedience, the word came to pass and the human race has been blessed ever since.

THE VALUE OF PROPHECY

Prophecy is a tremendous gift that God has given to His Church. It is full of tremendous benefits both individually and corporately. Here is a list of some of the values of receiving this gift into our lives and churches.

1. Prophecy brings healing. Proverbs 25:11 says, "A word fitly spoken is like apples of gold in settings of silver." Accepting the comfort and edification available through prophecy can heal a broken heart. As Graham Cooke writes,

Hurts, wounds, rejections and emotional trauma are a part of our lives, both before and after salvation. The Good News is that we serve a God who is committed to our healing at every level (physical, mental, and emotional). The goal of God is wholeness of life and fullness of the Spirit. Prophecy is a wonderful part of that healing and renewing process. Prophecy brings us, by direct verbal communication, into contact with God's real perspective on our lives and current situations.[4]

2. Prophecy deepens our relationship with God. When we ponder how the God of all creation cares enough to send a personal message from His heart, no matter what the function of the prophecy, it causes us to stop and think about what our individual value to Him must be! Receiving His word brings a new appreciation of God's deep love and care for us. It reminds us of our position with Him. As in any relationship, communication is key to reaching deeper levels. When God communicates with us, and we respond to Him, our relationship becomes deeper and more meaningful.

3. Prophecy provides direction and renewed vision. When we receive God's word, we often gain a clearer understanding of where He is leading us. Knowing where we are headed causes us to focus more intently on the plans and goals God has for us. New excitement and vision are often direct results of the prophetic word that brings us direction.

4. Prophecy brings biblical insight. As we will see in the next chapter, prophecy must line up with the written Word of God. This being the case, the revelation that comes through prophecy often opens up new insights and inspires deeper understanding of mysteries in the Bible. Paul says that we can gain "knowledge in the mystery of Christ, which in other ages was not made known to the sons of men, as it has now been revealed by the Spirit to His holy apostles and prophets" (Eph. 3:4-5). Prophecy often serves as a catalyst for understanding biblical truths that we have not seen or understood before.

5. Prophecy confirms. God uses a number of ways to communicate with us. It may come through reading Scripture or hearing a message or counseling a friend. God delights in confirming His message to us. He often uses prophecy to say something to us that we may have heard in some other form.

6. Prophecy warns. God does not want us ensnared by our own sin or by schemes of the devil. Prophecy, delivered in love, often warns us that our own sin will result in calamity and despair down the road if we do not repent and turn to God. Prophecy also warns us of traps the enemy has set for us. After the birth of Jesus, the wise men were warned not to return to Herod (see Matt. 2:12). Then Mary and Joseph were prophetically warned to flee to Egypt and stay there until the Lord spoke to them, in order to spare Jesus from Herod's plot to kill Him (see v. 13). Paul was warned by Jesus in Acts 22:18: "Make haste and get out of Jerusalem quickly, for they will not receive your testimony concerning Me." Because God sees the destiny He has for us, He often uses the prophetic word to warn us of the snares the enemy has set up to destroy our destined purposes.

7. Prophecy brings salvation. As I mentioned in chapter 1, when I was 11 years old, I clearly heard the voice of the Lord say, "This is your day." That was the day of my salvation. All salvation is a result of hearing the voice of the Lord on some level. Graham Cooke writes, "I have seen many atheists and agnostics persuaded by God through prophecy. It is the work of the Spirit to convict of sin (John 16:8-11). Prophecy can uncover past history which needs to be amended. It can provide an agenda for repentance, restitution, and revival."[5]

8. Prophecy releases new practices into the Church. There is nothing new under the sun, but there are diverse administrations. The administration of the thirteenth century will not work in the twenty-first century. By "new practices," I do not mean a departure from the Apostles' Creed. But there are new methods of operation and administration God is revealing to the Church that will burst us forth into new practices and new strategies that will work for the twenty-first century. Life means movement, so the minute we stop moving forward, we run the risk of facing death. Therefore, one of Satan's greatest strategies is to get us caught up in yesterday's methods. Prophecy breaks us out of the old methods and into new methods that are relevant for today.

9. Prophecy provides insight into counseling. When I am involved in a counseling situation, I rely on the prophetic voice of God to provide me with the understanding I need to give godly wisdom. The Lord often reveals to me what the problem is and what the root is, and then gives me a prophetic word to unlock the strategy that the person needs to move forward in God's plan for his or her life. It has proven to be a very effective method of counseling.

10. Prophecy shows us how to pray. At times our prayer lives can be stalled. Yet when we know the will of God in a certain area, we have great fuel for our prayer lives. God's will is made known to us through the prophetic. That knowledge gives us a basis for ongoing prayer to see His will done on Earth as it is in heaven.

11. Prophecy releases strategy for warfare. Praying through a prophetic word often entails spiritual warfare. First Timothy 1:18 says, "This charge I commit to you, son Timothy, according to the prophecies previously made concerning you, that by them you may wage the good warfare." Joshua also received prophetic instruction on the warfare he was to wage in order to see the walls of Jericho fall (see Josh. 6:1-5). Many times we see the enemy, but we don't wait for God's strategy to find out how to wage war against him. Prophecy provides us with the strategy we need to war against the enemy who strives to keep God's plans from manifesting in our lives. We often gain wisdom for knowing how to wage war.

12. Prophecy stirs faith. Prophecy can change things. When our spirits receive a word from the Lord, we know that there is hope and a way to see that prophetic word fulfilled. Remember how Jon was freed from alcoholism when Cindy gave him a redemptive prophecy? Jon's faith for seeing God deliver him and bring him into his destiny skyrocketed that day! That is the power of prophecy. In the next chapter, we will discuss the relationship between prophecy and faith in greater detail.

EZEKIEL AND THE FOUR STEPS TO FULFILLMENT

We must be in a perpetual process of receiving prophetic revelation. Our lives and destinies are on a continuum. As we move through life, we need to constantly seek new direction and revelation from God. We can't just grab ahold of one level of revelation and think that's going to get us through to the end.

In our book *The Best Is Yet Ahead*, Rebecca and I explain the four levels of prophecy that we see working in the life of Ezekiel in his vision of the Valley of Dry Bones (see Ezekiel 37). If Ezekiel had stopped at any point before God's full purpose had been accomplished, he would have failed. Ezekiel went through a four-step process at each new level of prophecy. These four steps are the same ones we need to follow if we are going to stay on track with prophetic fulfillment in our own lives.

Step One: He received prophetic revelation. Ezekiel sought God and was open to receiving prophetic instruction. In fact, he *expected* God to speak to him. How often in our daily lives do we *expect* to hear God? God is speaking to us today! We need to learn how to listen for God's voice and direction in our lives in order to receive the instructions that will move us forward.

Step Two: He obeyed the voice of the Lord. God told Ezekiel what to say and do in order for the next step to be accomplished. This seems so basic, and yet it is a critical step that we must understand. Ezekiel could not have moved to the complete fulfillment of prophecy without first obeying God at the first, second and third levels. If you are having difficulty gaining new revelation and hearing the voice of the Lord, go back and be sure you have done all that the Lord has required of you thus far. For example, if you have fallen out of relationship with someone and the Lord reveals to you that you need to make it right with that person, you should not go back to the Lord looking for new revelation until you have obeyed Him in the last revelation. If you want to continue to move forward toward prophetic fulfillment, you need to obey the current revelation and make it right with that person.

Step Three: He watched God's purpose being accomplished and assessed the situation. At each level of obedience, Ezekiel saw miracles happen as God's will was accomplished. Even so, he knew that all of God's purposes had not been fulfilled. When he prophesied to the dry bones as the Lord commanded him to do, he saw the bones come together. This in itself must have been a great and miraculous sight. But when he looked closer, he saw that even with this great miracle, there was no breath in the bones. When he again obeyed the Lord and prophesied, he saw breath come into the bones. A great army of living, breathing beings replaced a dead pile of dry, useless bones. And yet there was still hopelessness and infirmity. It was not until Ezekiel saw the Lord break infirmity and death off of the great army and bring them into the land He had promised them that the process of prophetic fulfillment was complete. Even though we may see great miracles along the way, we need to be sensitive to the Holy Spirit's leading as to whether or not His will has been fully accomplished.

Step Four: He listened for his next instruction. Miracle after miracle did not stop Ezekiel from seeking God for the next step. He did not bask in the awesome works of God in a way that stopped him from looking forward. Of course, we need to stop and thank God for His great power and allow ourselves to be drawn into worship, but we can't let the glory of something that already has occurred keep us from moving toward a greater level of glory.

Notes

1. J. D. Douglas, ed., *New Bible Dictionary* (Wheaton, IL: Tyndale House Publishers, 1982), n.p.
2. Dutch Sheets, *Watchman Prayer* (Ventura, CA: Gospel Light Publications, 2000), p. 29.
3. Graham Cooke, *Developing Your Prophetic Gifting* (Kent, England: Sovereign World Ltd., 1994), p. 119.
4. Ibid., pp. 30-31.
5. Ibid., pp. 39-40.

CHAPTER THREE

RECEIVING
THE WORD OF
THE LORD:

TESTING AND RESPONDING TO
A PROPHETIC WORD

We can receive a prophetic word from the Lord in many different ways: We may have an impression in our spirit; the Lord may illuminate a passage of Scripture that has particular significance in our lives; or we may have a vivid, prophetic dream. Prophecy can also come when someone communicates wisdom and counsel that gives others the direction they are looking for in their lives. Someone may even say, "I believe the Spirit of God is saying this to you." Prophecy can come from God or from angelic beings visiting you and giving you supernatural revelation. These are all sound, biblical methods that God uses at different times to speak to us.

PROPHECY HAS BOUNDARIES

We must be aware of several things as we begin to move into receiving prophetic words. We must understand that prophecy has boundaries that God has established for our own protection. For instance, in a corporate setting, Paul gives the following guideline: "Let two or three prophets speak, and let the others judge" (1 Cor. 14:29).

Another boundary is set in 1 Thessalonians 5:19-21, "Do not quench the Spirit. Do not despise prophecies. Test all things; hold fast what is good." The rest of this chapter is devoted to applying tests to prophetic words so that we can hold fast to what is good.

DETERMINING IF THE WORD IS FROM GOD

Not every voice we hear is from the Holy Spirit. Satan has the ability to counterfeit gifts in order to bring confusion and get us off course. His ability to counterfeit includes the gift of prophecy. Jeremiah records the Lord saying, "I have not sent these prophets, yet they ran. I have not spoken to them, yet they prophesied" (Jer. 23:21).

This still happens. There are false prophets. This is why we are admonished to test all things and hold on to what is good. Here are some unclean sources of prophetic words that we need to be aware of.

1. The occult. "You are wearied in the multitude of your counsels; let now the astrologers, the stargazers, and the monthly prognosticators stand up and save you from what shall come upon you" (Isa. 47:13). Occultic sources of prophecy include psychics, tarot cards, Ouija boards, astrology and horoscopes, clairvoyants, mediums, ESP, witchcraft, divination and so forth. These sources of prophetic utterance must be avoided completely! Saul, for example, gained revelation by visiting a witch. However, because it was an illegitimate source of revelation—not from God—it ultimately resulted in Saul's death.

2. Delusions. "How long will this be in the heart of the prophets who prophesy lies? Indeed they are prophets of the deceit of their own heart" (Jer. 23:26). Not everyone that gives you a false prophecy is malicious; they are just confused. Sometimes they are walking in their own delusion, thinking they are hearing God when they are not.

3. Unrestrained desires. Desires are a natural function of the human emotion. Desires are linked with our wishes, aspirations, urges and expectations. Gone unchecked, desires can cause us to rebel against the will of God in our lives. Have you ever heard anyone use the expression "yearning desire"? Many times we can so yearn to have something that we listen for any voice that will align with our desires. False prophecy can, therefore, come through a desire so unrestrained that we can no longer discern the voice of the Lord over the voice of the enemy or our own flesh. Prophecy can come out of the longings of someone's heart, rather than from a pure word from the Lord.

4. Manipulation and control. "Likewise, son of man, set your face against the daughters of your people, who prophesy out of their own heart; prophesy against them" (Ezek. 13:17). Prophecy has been used to try to manipulate people into taking actions that they might not take otherwise. For instance, someone might want a certain person to marry another person. It seems like a good thing—so good, in fact, that God must want it, too—so they go up to one or the other and say, "The Lord says you are to marry _____." The true origin behind the word was not God but a manipulative and controlling spirit. We will discuss this further later in the chapter.

5. Immaturity. There are true prophets who have not yet matured in their gifting and may deliver a word from the Lord mixed with their own emotions. Therefore, the word is impure. This is where some sifting needs to take place and where we need to "hold fast what is good."

6. False dreams. "Behold, I am against those who prophesy false dreams" (Jer. 23:32). The enemy is able to counterfeit prophetic dreams, just as he is able to counterfeit prophetic words. We must realize that when we are asleep, we are not fully active in our spirit. Many times the enemy will use this time to speak false words to us.

7. Demons. "And I have seen folly in the prophets of Samaria: they prophesied by Baal and caused My people Israel to err" (Jer. 23:13). Just as the Lord can send angels to prophesy, the enemy can send one of his hosts (Baal was sent in the biblical example given) to deliver a demonic prophecy.

JUDGING PROPHECY

There are many origins for what may seem like prophecy from God. How do we know if what is being said is from God? How do we test prophecy? The following list has been compiled part-ly from Graham Cooke's *Developing Your Prophetic Gifting* and partly from my own experience in judging prophecy:

1. Does the word you have received edify, exhort and comfort you? Does it accomplish the basic functions we out-lined in the last chapter? First Corinthians 14:3 says that the real purpose of prophecy is to edify, exhort and comfort. If the word leaves you with a sense of uneasiness instead of edification, or if you feel that something is just not right, you should not receive the word without further testing.

2. What is the spirit behind the prophecy? Someone might begin to speak a word to you, but the spirit behind the word does not seem right. It may have a spirit of condemnation on it. Even though it could be totally true, if you feel weighted down and condemned, you may need to judge it further. Remember, the spirit in which all prophecy should be given is love. Therefore, even a word of exhortation or correction should leave you with a freedom to rebuild.

3. Does it conform to Scripture? God is not going to say one thing in the Bible and then tell you the opposite in a prophetic word. The prophetic word of the Lord will *always* line up with the inspired, written Word of God, which has been given to us as a guide and an example. Remember, the Bible has no bounds or time frame; therefore, you will find that the principles and the illumination of the Word of God are just as important for us today as they were when it was written. In other words, your exam-ple or Scriptural principle may be found in the Old Testament as often as in the New Testament. But if someone gives you a word and you find no Scriptural principle, basis or example for it in the Bible, you should not fully embrace the word.

4. Does it display the character of Christ? In *The Voice of God*, Cindy Jacobs says, "Sometimes wolves in sheep's clothing manip-ulate Scripture for their own purposes. Just because someone is quoting chapter and verse to you doesn't make a prophecy accurate. Even if Scripture is being used, another area to check is to make sure Christ's character shines through the prophetic word."[1] This, again, leads to love. In addition to love, prophetic words should exalt Jesus rather than a person or ministry. They should lead us to His feet rather than to an organization.

5. Is it manipulative or controlling? Even though some words are filled with truth, they can be used by the one giving the word to manipulate or control others. Control and manipulation are used to wield power, abuse, dominate or rule over others. Such a word has no love, much less any of the other fruit of the spirit, and should be discarded.

6. Does it usurp your will? Does the word say you *must* do this or that? Does it overpower you in such a way that you are not able to exercise your own free will to choose what you will do? If so, that should be a red flag. God gives us all freedom—even the freedom to sin. All prophetic words should leave you the choice to either accept them or reject them.

7. Does it pull rank? In other words, does the word begin to move you out of the authority structure in which God has placed you? Does it breed rebellion against authority or produce suspicion or insubordination? Does it pull you out of the place God has you spiritually? God gave each of His children an authority structure in which to operate. If the word suggests that you supersede biblical authority, reject it!

8. Does it confirm what God is saying to you? God is always willing to confirm His word to you. When God gives a word, He will usually give it over and over again in many forms. Prophetic words often confirm what God has already spoken to you and fit in with what He is doing in your life.

9. Does it allow outside perspective? If someone gives you a word and says that you are not supposed to communicate it with anyone else, be careful. This is a violation of Scripture. First

Thessalonians 5:21 tells us that any word of God is to be evaluated. Godly council is always in order when you receive a word, particularly when it tells you to do something drastic, like quit your job and move to another city. Proverbs 11:14 tells us there is wisdom in a multitude of counselors, which includes judging the prophetic. In fact, a good test of any prophecy is to take it to a mature spiritual friend or authority figure in your life and ask him or her to help you judge the word.

10. Does it give a dire warning? Warnings are fine, but see what kind of a warning it is. Is the warning so dire that you have no way out, producing hopelessness in you? Or does the warning show you your way of escape? Is there redemption? Cindy Jacobs tells the story of one such warning that I prophesied over Houston, Texas, on September 21, 1994:

> *I would say, the next 24 days are critical.* Though the enemy has stood against you as a city, I have brought you to a crossroads and you are about to make a transition and crossover. My eyes are upon this city and the remnant of this city, and I will overcome the structures that are set against My Spirit in this city. Revelation that has been withheld is going to begin to come down to people like rain. *Look to the river of the east.* As that river rises so will My people.
>
> Watchman, what do you see? He replied, "*I see a fire. It is a literal fire. Fire is on the river.*" Then the Lord said, "My fire will begin to come to this city."
>
> "I would call you to the night watch. Gather together in the night watch. Sing in the night in the hard areas of the city and evil will be uncovered and deliverance will come. If you will enter into the night watch, you will overthrow the impending destruction and doom that is set for the area."

One of the prayer leaders, Deborah DeGar, took the prophetic word from church to church, leading a prayer watch from 3:00 to 6:00 A.M. *At the end of 24 days, it began to rain in Houston.* There had never been a flood exactly like it in the history of the city. Houston was brought before the eyes of the nation. The San Jacinto River *(the river to the east)* began to rise and flood the entire territory. Gas lines erupted underneath the river and the flooded river *literally had a fire that burned in its midst.* In the middle of the chaos, the Church came together in great unity.

In the case of this prophetic warning, the flooding was not averted, but it did not do the damage it could have done.[2]

11. How do you feel about the word in your spirit? God has given each of us discernment in our spirits. If we receive a prophetic word and it just doesn't seem right to us for whatever reason, we have cause to check it out further before we embrace it as a word from the Lord.

12. Is it confirmed by the Church? If a word is given in a corporate setting, there should be instant feedback from the people and the leaders. There should be a corporate "amen" that comes forth. Rebecca Sytsema, my co-author, was once in a meeting in the Anaheim Vineyard when a man stood up during worship to give a prophetic word. He said that the Lord was longing to fulfill the desire of His children's hearts. He said that God was, in fact, a God who longed to bring even what seemed like fairy tales to pass. He finished his word and sat down. When worship concluded, John Wimber came to the microphone. After a moment of silence, he simply stated, "Our God is *not* a fairy-tale God!" A loud round of applause went up from the crowd, many of whom had discerned that something had not been right with the word. If a word is given in a corporate setting, what is the reaction of the leaders and the congregation?

13. Does it come to pass? "When a prophet speaks in the name of the LORD, if the thing does not happen or come to pass, that is the thing which the LORD has not spoken; the prophet has spoken it presumptuously" (Deut. 18:22). Here is, of course, one of the most basic tests of a prophetic word. Remember, prophecy may be conditional, based upon something we must do. If you read through the list of responses in the next chapter and are satisfied that you have done all that God has required of you concerning the word, but it is still not fulfilled, it may not have been a word from the Lord at all.

14. Does it produce fruit? A true word from the Lord will bear good fruit that you will be able to discern. In his book *Prophecy*, Bruce Yocum writes,

> If we pay attention to the effect that prophetic utterances have, we can judge their worth. A word from the Lord will produce life, peace, hope, love, and all the other fruit of the Holy Spirit. A word which is not from the Lord will either produce the fruit of evil—strife, anger, jealousy, lust, indifference—or it will have no effect at all.[3]

What kind of fruit has been produced in your life by the prophetic word? This will be a telling factor in whether or not you accept it as a word from the Lord.

RESPONDING TO PROPHECY

Once we have tested a prophetic word and have come to the conclusion that God has spoken into our lives, we must then understand how to respond to what we have been told. Here is a helpful checklist of proper actions to take.

1. Keep a journal. There is tremendous importance in writing down, tape-recording or keeping some kind of record of prophetic words. We can't rely purely on our memories. Having a record of prophecy helps us remember the whole word, keeps us from adding thoughts to the word, and builds our faith when we go back and read the word. We can also see how the word we received fits in with what God has said to us in the past.

There are times, however, when we do not clearly understand all that God is trying to say to us at the time the word is given. Having a record of the word helps us go back and gain fresh understanding at a later time. For example, in June of 1998, I was given a birthday party at the home of C. Peter Wagner. Cindy Jacobs had come to help celebrate. During the party, Cindy began to feel a spirit of prophecy come upon her. Peter, who keeps a full prophetic journal, grabbed a tape recorder. Cindy gave me a beautiful word for the new year I was entering into in my own life. Then she turned to Peter and began to prophesy that God was calling him to raise up a seminary that would gather leaders from around the world. She went on to give several specific details.

At the time, such a thought had never entered Peter's mind. He had no frame of reference for such a concept. Nonetheless, Cindy's word was transcribed and entered on page 67 of the Wagner Prophetic Journal. A few months later, Peter met with several apostles from various streams of Christianity. During that meeting, the Lord spoke to Peter about a whole new concept for training leaders from around the world. It became clear that he was to retire from his position as a professor at Fuller Theological Seminary, where he had taught for 30 years, and begin his own seminary-type school. As he obeyed the Lord, God began pouring new revelation out as to how the school would operate. Later that year, he officially formed Wagner Leadership Institute, and the first student was enrolled that December.

Peter was able to go back to page 67 of his journal and revisit exactly what the Lord had spoken to him. In fact, as he began to seek counsel and set up the leadership for the school, he was able to distribute copies of the word Cindy had given him so that those involved would also know the word God had given over the new venture.

2. Do not interpret the word by the desires of your flesh. Many of God's people have fallen into deception by taking a prophetic word and adding their own interpretation to it, then saying that God promised them this or that. Cindy Jacobs offers the following caution:

> I have had many singles come to me saying God has promised them certain mates because they were told so in prophecies. When I asked them what the prophecies said, they came up with something like, "God said He would give me the desires of my heart and so-and-so is the desire of my heart." [Such an interpretation] may be the desire of their flesh but God may not have anything to do with it at all.[4]

Be very careful not to take a word and run in a direction God has not ordained.

3. Embrace the word. To embrace means to grab hold of something. When we embrace or grab hold of a word, it activates faith to see the word fulfilled. Remember, "faith comes by hearing, and hearing by the word of God" (Rom. 10:17). When we embrace a true prophetic word, it brings faith that God has a destiny for us. We must allow ourselves to embrace our prophetic word with the faith that God is well able to do what He said He would do. If God has inspired the word, He will uphold it by the Holy Spirit. Even if we have received a difficult word, if the word is from God, faith will rise within our spirit, because we know that God has a path for us.

When I was 18, the Lord spoke to me and said, "I have called you for the healing of the nations." At that time, the only frame of reference I had for a call to the nations was to become a missionary, which was something I did not want to do. Even though I was willing to obey God, I did not embrace His word to me. It was 10 years later when God spoke that word to me again. This time I embraced the word fully. He then began to show me that He had not called me to be a missionary, but rather an intercessor, prophet and strategist for the nations He would lay on my heart. He began to open doors for me to travel in and out of nations so that I could bring prophetic words and build up strategic intercession to see His will accomplished. Had I not been willing to embrace this word when He spoke it to me a second time, I would have missed that portion of His destiny for my life.

4. Pray it through. Because prophecy is provisional, once we know what God wants to do in our lives, the best thing to do is to begin to pray along those lines. This will not only help to build our relationship to God and persistence in faith, it will also teach us spiritual warfare. The enemy does not want to see God's will accomplished in our lives; he will do all he can to see that we are not successful in reaching our destinies. That is why we must commit ourselves to praying through the word until we see it come to pass. For instance, I have known many barren couples who have received words about children. Yet they did not conceive immediately. In some cases, it took years. But as they chose to pray through their word with the faith that God is well able to do all that He says, the bondage of barrenness broke off their physical bodies and often their spiritual lives as well.

5. Obey the word. As previously mentioned, prophecy is often provisional, which means we must do something to see it come to pass. There are conditions to meet. Here is a good biblical example: "*If* My people who are called by My name will humble themselves, and pray and seek My face, and turn from their wicked ways, *then* I will hear from heaven, and will forgive their sin and heal their land" (2 Chron. 7:14, emphasis added). Does God want to forgive the sin and heal the land of His people? Of course! But they have to do something in order to see that prophecy occur—namely, humble themselves, pray, seek His face and turn from their wicked ways. Something that has been prophesied to us may never come to pass if we are not faithful to meet the conditions.

In chapter 2, I told the story of how God gave a clear word of direction to Rebecca, instructing her to go to the conference in California in order to meet Jack. Had she not gone to that conference, she could have missed meeting God's chosen mate for her. God surely could have arranged another way for them to meet, but there was a timing issue involved as well. Her obedience to the prophetic word kept her moving forward in God's timing and destiny for her life.

6. Look for the fulfillment of the word. Having completed steps one through five, we should look for and expect that the word will be fulfilled. John 1:14 speaks of the word becoming flesh, which is a good statement for the fulfillment of a prophetic word. God desires that His word be made flesh—that the intangible substance of a prophetic promise becomes a tangible reality in our lives. Many do not see their promise manifested because they do not know how to watch for the fulfillment of their word.

CAN WE PROPHESY?

While it is not within the scope of this book to thoroughly answer this question, the discussion of prophecy would not be complete without a brief look at who can prophesy. While not all of us are called as God's spokespersons on the earth, the fact is that we all prophesy, whether it is through sharing an encouraging word, edifying a friend, giving godly advice or knowingly giving a prophetic word. Romans 12:6 says we prophesy according to our measure of faith. What measure of faith are you operating in? I want to encourage you to ask God right now to increase your faith.

If you are a believer in the Lord Jesus Christ, the Holy Spirit is made resident within you. You can now ask the Spirit of God to begin to speak through you, with the knowledge that He can. You can also give Him liberty to begin to manifest His particular giftings within you, whether they are in prophecy, helping, hospitality, teaching or any of the gifts listed in Romans 12, 1 Corinthians 12 and Ephesians 4. All the gifts are greatly needed in the body of Christ—including yours!

Notes
1. Cindy Jacobs, *The Voice of God* (Ventura, CA: Regal Books, 1995), p. 76.
2. Ibid., p. 181.
3. Bruce Yocum, *Prophecy* (Ann Arbor, MI: Servant Publications, 1976), p. 119.
4. Jacobs, *The Voice of God,* pp. 83-84.

CHAPTER FOUR

WALKING IN REVELATION

That the God of our Lord Jesus Christ, the Father of glory,
may give to you the spirit of wisdom and revelation in the knowledge
of Him, the eyes of your understanding being enlightened; that you may
know what is the hope of His calling, what are the riches of the
glory of His inheritance in the saints.

EPHESIANS   1:17-18

When God speaks to us, whether by prophecy or any number of other means, His purpose in doing so is to bring a new level of revelation to our lives. Revelation is essential for living a victorious Christian life. We need the Spirit of wisdom and revelation in order to accomplish the hope of God's calling over our lives. We need God not only to reveal what our next step should be, but also the snares the enemy has set for us on the road ahead so that we can walk in wisdom.

"Revelation" means to manifest, make clear, show forth, unfold, explain by narration, instruct, admonish, warn or give an answer to a question. When God speaks to us, He brings one or more of these aspects of revelation so that the eyes of our minds may be enlightened to who He is. Throughout the Bible, God actively disclosed Himself to humanity, and He has not wavered in His desire for us to understand Him. He continues to reveal His power, glory, nature, character, will, ways, plans and strategies to His people today.

Revelation from God has three important functions in our lives, as follows:

1. **Revelation causes obscure things to become clear.** Jeremiah 33:3 says, "Call to Me and I will answer you and show you great and mighty things, fenced in and hidden, which you do not know (do not distinguish and recognize, have knowledge of and understand)" (*AMP*).

2. **Revelation brings hidden things to light.** One important definition of "revelation" is "apocalypse," which means to unveil or reveal something that is hidden so that it may be seen and known for what it is. We need this kind of revelation in our lives to understand how to overcome Satan's attempts to thwart God's plan for our lives.

3. **Revelation shows signs that will point us into our paths of destiny.** We need revelation in order to know God's will for our lives and, as we come into agreement with His will, how to walk it out. Revelation is not a one-time deal. We need fresh revelation on a continual basis in order to keep moving forward in God's plan and timing.

GAINING REVELATION

These three functions of revelation help us understand the "why," but an even bigger question is "how." To answer that question, let's look at Ephesians 1:20-23:

> Which He worked in Christ when He raised Him from the dead and seated Him at His right hand in the heavenly places, far above all principality and power and might and dominion, and every name that is named, not only in this age but also in that which is to come. And He put all things under His feet, and gave Him to be head over all things to the church, which is His body, the fullness of Him who fills all in all.

This passage tells us that Jesus is able to defeat the enemy's structures in our lives from His position as "head over all things," because all things are under His feet. Because Jesus is head, we need to think the way He thinks and put on the mind of Christ (see 1 Cor. 2:16). Our cognitive processes must align with the thoughts of God in order to be successful in the earth realm.

The problem is that our minds are naturally at enmity with God because of our flesh. We must find a way, therefore, to go beyond our brains and move to a place where we have put on the mind of Christ; a place where the Spirit of wisdom and revelation has been activated in our lives. To do this, we need to move into that realm of faith in which God will be able to show us new revelation in a way that we, as individuals, can receive it. The first important step in gaining revelation is to believe that God has revelation for us and that He has a way to communicate it to us. The second step is to be open and aware of what God is saying. The third step is to enter into a new faith realm.

FAITH COMES BY HEARING, AND HEARING BY THE WORD OF GOD!

Faith is the general persuasion of the mind that a certain statement is true. The primary idea behind faith is trust. When we believe that something is true, it is worthy of our trust. Romans 10:16-17 says, "But they have not all obeyed the gospel. For Isaiah says, 'LORD, who has believed our report?' So then faith comes by hearing, and hearing by the word of God."

The Holy Spirit uses the Word of God to awaken a response of faith within us. Our trust in the Word of God is the stable ground on which we stand for salvation. A response of faith produces certain characteristics within us. Here is a list of the characteristics of faith and each one's opposite quality.

Trust vs. *Mistrust*
Belief vs. *Unbelief*
Loyalty vs. *Betrayal*
Fidelity vs. *Unfaithfulness*
Confidence vs. *Insecurity*
Obedience vs. *Disobedience*
Wholeness vs. *Fragmentation*

When I hear a word that I believe is from the Lord or feel that the Spirit of God is quickening His voice within me, I weigh what I hear based on the characteristics of faith. When I hear a voice that represents the opposite of faith to me, I reject that voice. God has given us each a measure of faith. Romans 12:6 says, "Having then gifts differing according to the grace that is given us, let us use them: if prophecy, *let us prophesy in proportion to our faith*" (emphasis added). Our faith should be ever growing and becoming stronger.

The concept of faith is the keynote, central Christian message. Based upon our faith, we enter into the state of salvation (see Eph. 2:8-9); our sanctification is linked to faith (see Acts 26:18); our continuing purification is a result of our faith (see Acts 15:9); and we are justified by faith (see Rom. 4:5; 5:1). Thank the Lord that we are adopted by Him and through faith gain a supernatural faith structure (see Rom. 8:15; Gal. 3:26). Faith is also called a fruit of the spirit. Fruit is something that can be created and seen in a person (see Gal. 5:22-23). Faith is also a supernatural gift that gives us the ability to do great acts for God. Jesus said that through faith we can move mountains (see Matt. 17:20; 1 Cor. 13:2).

RECEIVING REVELATION

As we mentioned earlier, the primary way God speaks to us on a regular basis is through Scripture. He may use a verse or passage to bring great revelation for a specific situation in our lives. But not everyone who reads the Bible gains revelation. Some read it purely for historical value. Others read it in the same way they would a Chinese proverb—for principles and insight, but nothing more. However, a Christian, in whom the Spirit of God is alive and active, can read the same passages and gain incredible, tremendous insight and hear the "now" voice of God for their lives.

Four Greek words describe the functions of the Word of God—how different individuals can read the same passage of Scripture, but each individual receives something different:

1. Graphe. This is the written, historical Word of God. Anyone, saved or not, can read and understand the Bible from this perspective. Reading the Bible as *graphe* is like reading a novel. You understand the story and possibly even the historical value, and maybe ponder the characters and settings, but really glean little else.

2. Logos. This is seeing the meaning of the principles of the Bible. For instance, it includes understanding the personal value of following the Golden Rule or reaping what has been sown. These are generally good life principles to follow, but can be of value whether saved or unsaved.

3. Rhema. This is where the Word of God crosses over into revelation. *Rhema* is when the *graphe* and *logos* are illuminated to you by the Holy Spirit. *Rhema* brings enlightenment and bears witness in your spirit. No one who is truly saved has been saved without a *rhema* understanding of their need for Christ in their lives.

4. Zoe. All Christians have received a *rhema* word from God, or they could not have come into salvation. For some, their revelation from God ends there. However, for those who walk in the Spirit of wisdom and revelation, reading the Word of God becomes a creative, living part of who they are. When the Word of God becomes *zoe*, it dwells within them. The *rhema* becomes sustained, life-giving revelation. God has clear channels to speak revelation to those who read the Bible as *zoe* life.

Having looked at the different functions of the Bible, let's look at one way to move from reading the Bible as *graphe* to gaining *zoe* revelation. Let's take Jeremiah 33:3 as an example:

Call to Me and I will answer you and show you great and mighty things, fenced in and hidden, which you do not know (do not distinguish and recognize, have knowledge of and understand) (*AMP*).

Read it out loud. Then write out the Scripture, outlining the main points. For example:

1. Call to Me
2. I will answer you
3. Show you great and mighty things, fenced in and hidden

Then ask God to activate the Spirit of wisdom and revelation in you regarding that passage. Ask Him to show you things that go beyond your brain and things that you do not currently distinguish or recognize. Ask Him to show you things that you have not seen before. Write down any and all impressions you receive as you are meditating on the Scripture. You may want to do this on more than one occasion. As you allow yourself to receive the impressions, trust the impressions enough to write them down, and allow faith, which God is speaking to you, to arise within you. When it becomes alive and you start seeing *rhema* revelation that you have not seen before, ask God how it applies to you and your situation. Ask Him to establish the *rhema* within you, so that it becomes ongoing, sustained *zoe* life.

Of course, we can hear God in many different ways, and God may bring us *zoe* revelation without going through this process. But for those who are not used to receiving revelation from God, this simple formula is one place to start.

SOME WAYS GOD SPEAKS

Hearing the voice of God and receiving revelation is not as difficult as some might think. Many of God's people hear Him, but have not learned how to perceive His voice. As we have said before, to perceive means to take hold of, feel, comprehend, grasp mentally, recognize, observe or discern. Learning to perceive God's voice and act upon it is a key to living a successful

We should never underestimate the power of Scripture as an instrument of God to speak to us in a personal way.

Christian life. How does God speak to us? There are several ways. While this list is not exhaustive, it shows some of the ways God speaks to His people today.

1. The Bible. We have said this before, but it bears repeating: The first and foremost way we hear God speak to us is through the Bible—Holy Scripture, which is His written revelation to humanity. When reading the Bible, has a verse ever just seemed to jump off the page? When that happens, it is often God communicating a particular truth to us for our particular situation. We should never underestimate the power of Scripture as an instrument of God to speak to us in a personal way. In fact, the Bible is our litmus test for any other kind of revelation we feel we are receiving. If we think we have heard God, but what we hear contradicts the Bible in any way, we can be sure it's not God's voice we are hearing!

2. God's still, small voice. When God speaks to us in this way, we know something is right. We have a strong feeling to move ahead in one direction, or we find an issue in our heart has been settled and the answer is clear to us. Some may call this intuition or even a sixth sense, but it is often an inaudible voice of God speaking directly into our spirits.

3. Other people. God can and often does speak a very direct prophetic word to us through other people. Some biblical examples include

- King David expressing, "The Spirit of the LORD spoke through me; his word was on my tongue" (2 Sam. 23:2, *NIV*).
- Peter saying, "But men spoke from God as they were carried along by the Holy Spirit" (2 Pet. 1:21, *NIV*).

This can happen in the preaching and teaching we receive, in conversations we have with others, in the prophetic word or a word of knowledge or wisdom we receive, or through tongues and interpretation. No matter the method, when the Lord uses someone to speak His words to us, they hit us in a deep and profound way—like someone turning on the lights in the midst of darkness.

4. God's creation. "For since the creation of the world God's invisible qualities—his eternal power and divine nature—have been clearly seen, being understood from what has been made, so that men are without excuse" (Rom. 1:20, *NIV*). Have you ever felt the presence of God in a sunset, a flower or even a raging thunderstorm? At times, great beauty in nature or even in a moral truth can be a vehicle for a direct word from God. In the Bible, God used a rainbow as a sign of His covenant with Noah (see Gen. 9:9-17). He used dew on a fleece to help guide Gideon (see Judg. 6:36-40). He caused a fig tree that did not bear fruit to wither and die (see Matt. 21:19-21). The righteousness He makes available to you is likened throughout Scripture to white snow (see Isa. 1:18). If you take the time to stop and look around you, you may be surprised to find that God speaks through His creation.

5. Dreams and visions. "'We both had dreams,' they answered, 'but there is no one to interpret them.' Then Joseph said to them, 'Do not interpretations belong to God? Tell me your dreams'" (Gen. 40:8, *NIV*). We see many biblical examples of God speaking to His people in dreams and visions. He spoke to Joseph, Solomon, Pharaoh, many prophets and kings, and Joseph (Jesus' earthly father) by this means. Joel 2:28 says, "And afterward, I will pour out my Spirit on all people. . . . your old men will dream dreams, your young men will see visions" (*NIV*). God still speaks through dreams today. If we awake from a dream that seems unusually vivid and very real, we may want to ask the Lord if He is trying to speak something to us through that dream. We will take a much closer look at this in the next two chapters.

6. Experiences or circumstances. There may be times when God speaks to us through very specific incidents. Sometimes this happens in prayer at home. Sometimes this happens when we respond to an altar call. Often this will occur when people first become saved. It may be a moment when tremendous clarity comes as a result of some incident. When God speaks to us through a specific experience, we will be able to point back to that moment in time as a benchmark for a shifting in our lives. Many times perplexing circumstances arise in our lives. However, we need to look deep into these circumstances so we can hear clearly God's voice.

7. Angels. Throughout the Bible, God sent angels as His messengers to speak something to His people. This method of communication is still one He chooses to use from time to time, and it's one that you cannot discount. One day God may surprise you!

8. Audible voice. Sometimes God chooses to speak in an audible voice. He did so to young Samuel as well as to many others in the Bible. Genesis tells us that it was by His audible voice that God created all of heaven, Earth and every creature that has breath. Can God not use that same voice to speak to His creation?

BARRIERS TO REVELATION

Looking at some of the ways God speaks to us poses the question, Why don't we hear Him more often? Of course, God can choose when, where, how and to whom He will speak. But assuming that He attempts to communicate with us, what are some of the issues in our lives that can prevent us from gaining revelation? Here is a list of some barriers many of us have dealt with or are dealing with today.

1. Distractions. Have you ever found it difficult to pray? Or once you set your mind to it, you became bored and distracted? We often miss what God may be trying to say to us simply because we are unable to focus on Him. If we are having a phone conversation with someone while trying to do three other things, chances are we don't absorb all of the conversation. This is one of the reasons why we are exhorted by Scripture to meditate on God and His Word. If we can find a strategy to minimize our distractions, we may be amazed to hear God speaking to us.[1]

2. Disinformation. Often, as Christians, we look to our churches and our colleagues to build our theology rather than base our doctrinal stand on what God's Word says. This is why many have come to believe that God does not speak to His children today—not because of anything the Bible has said, but because of disinformation they have received somewhere along the line. God has given us His Word and His promises, and He expects us to check our decisions and our beliefs with Scripture so that we will not get tripped up with disinformation. We are always correct to ask God to renew our minds so that we conform to Him rather than to the beliefs of the world (see Rom. 12:2).[2]

3. Disbelief. Many cannot and will not hear the voice of God in their lives because they simply do not believe. They may have come to salvation and even pray from time to time, but they really expect little or nothing to come of it. If we truly believed that every time we pray, God—who has control of everything in and around us—not only listens to us, but also desires to converse with us, we would pray every chance we got. However, because we often don't see immediate (or what we consider to be adequate) answers to our prayers, we fall into unbelief. We must remember that we serve an all-powerful, all-knowing God who we can trust to give us the very best in spite of what we ask for or in spite of how we interpret His answer. If we have fallen into unbelief, our first prayer back toward God should be, "I do believe; help me overcome my unbelief!" (Mark 9:24, *NIV*).[3]

In our book *Possessing Your Inheritance*, Rebecca and I point out the following progression that can lead to missing God's revelation. When God does speak, we must realize that we have an enemy who immediately tries to steal from us what is rightfully ours. Satan will always attempt to thwart God's plans. Such was the case for the Israelites. When they were coming out of their captivity in Babylon, they received a revelation from the Lord (see Jer. 29:10). The Israelites knew God's will for them was to return and rebuild the destroyed Temple of the Lord. They had heard clearly from God. But as they began working toward the restoration God had for them, the enemy resisted their efforts. Instead of fighting for what they knew they were to do, the children of Israel gave in. As the people allowed the enemy to take a foothold, three things happened.

1. **They fell into *discouragement*.** They began to ask why God was calling them to rebuild the Temple in the first place.

2. **They fell into *disillusionment.*** Things weren't going well, so they began to wonder if God had really told them to build at all.

3. **They fell into *disinterest.*** As the situation progressed, they decided they would build their own houses and leave His in disrepair. They stopped caring.

This progression of events is often a pattern for what can happen in our own lives if we do not guard what the Lord has told us and seriously pursue His will. It takes an act of our own will to choose God's plan for possessing our inheritance.[4]

PROCESSING REVELATION

God had a purpose in having the Israelites rebuild His Temple. It was not because God was being selfish. Rebuilding had a direct effect on restoring to the Israelites what had been lost through their captivity in Babylon. It was important for their future. When God brings revelation into our lives, it is not an end in itself. Instead, it is part of a process intended to move us toward our potential and our destiny. In this book, we have looked at the value of prophecy in our lives. Prophecy, as well as the majority of revelation we receive, moves us through the following process:

1. **God tells us about Himself.** Often, God will use the Bible as His means of communicating with us about who He is. Even when He uses other methods, they will always align with what the Bible says. Therefore, it is imperative that we become as familiar as we can with the Word of God.

2. **God tells us what He has planned.**

3. **God tells us that we are a part of the plan.**

Not everyone is open to receiving what God has to say. This is because whenever revelation comes from God, it directly confronts us. When we are confronted with truth from God, we must deal with it on some level. Revelation from God requires a response. While God is sovereign, we must respond to His sovereignty in order for His will to be done.

God's revelation comes to us not as information for our brains to process, but as a mandate for our faith to arise and as a guide to conduct our lives. Without faith it is impossible to please God. Equally true, however, is that faith without actions is dead. Revelation challenges us on both levels. Once we gain revelation, we are obligated to that revelation. We become accountable for what God has revealed to us. In order to reach our destiny, we must receive revelation from God and then act accordingly. Of course, sometimes the most appropriate reaction is to wait on God with expectancy, but the principle remains the same. It is when we do not act upon the revelation we receive that windows of opportunity can close—sometimes forever. Walking in revelation and reaching our destiny in God can be summed up very simply. In every circumstance in which we find ourselves, we must find God's sovereign plan within that circumstance and be faithful to walk in His will.

Notes

1. Marilyn Willett Heavilin, *I'm Listening, Lord* (Nashville, TN: Thomas Nelson Publishers, 1993), pp. 33-37.
2. Ibid., pp. 49-51.
3. Ibid., pp. 54-57.
4. Chuck D. Pierce and Rebecca Wagner Sytsema, *Possessing Your Inheritance* (Ventura, CA: Renew Books, 1999), pp. 100-101.

CHAPTER FIVE

HEARING GOD THROUGH DREAMS AND VISIONS

Then He said, If there is a prophet among you, I, the LORD, make Myself known to him in a vision; I speak to him in a dream.

N U M B E R S   1 2 : 6

We concluded the last chapter by saying that in every circumstance in which we find ourselves, we must find God's sovereign plan within that circumstance and be faithful to walk in His will. One of the primary ways God communicates with His people is through dreams and visions, yet those dreams and visions are often misunderstood, dismissed or ignored. Dreams particularly can seem foolish or strange. But as Ira Milligan points out,

> Paul said that God chose the foolish things of the world to confound the wise (see 1 Cor. 1:27). Although many dreams are foolish or senseless to the world, they are precious to those who understand "the hidden wisdom" from above (1 Cor. 2:7).[1]

Fiona Starr and Jonny Zucker point out,

> The Old Testament is laden with dream scenes and interpretations. One of the best known is the story of Jacob's son, Joseph. Joseph was said to hold the power of forecasting through his dreams. Joseph's dream analyses were often the cause of much sibling rivalry, not only because of the unique power that Joseph possessed, but also because of the content of the dreams. In many of his dreams Joseph dreamt of himself as the superior brother. The others grew angry with Joseph's seeming arrogance and tried to exile him while convincing Jacob that his favorite son was dead. Joseph's power, however, helped him find his way out of a dangerous situation when he was able to help Pharaoh of Egypt interpret his own dreams.
>
> Jacob's ladder is another well-known biblical dream story. Some say that the dream of the ladder resting on

earth but leading up to the heavens is a symbol for higher communication between God and humans on earth.[2]

The Lord uses dreams and visions to guide, warn, direct, help and communicate His heart. God has not stopped communicating to humanity by these means.

In the Bible, there are over 50 references for God sending messages through dreams and visions to both the righteous and the unrighteous. The Lord used dreams and visions to guide, warn, direct, help and communicate His heart. God has not stopped communicating to humanity by these means. In fact, God often uses dreams and visions to reach unsaved individuals with the gospel, particularly in closed parts of the world. In Global Harvest Ministries, where I serve as vice president, we recently reported one such story:

An Iranian living near Kassel told a Christian worker of a dream he recently had: "I was standing on the roof of my house when a bright light like a spotlight shone on me. This light then moved down to illuminate a stream, which seemed to be made of light. I don't know what it means. I have consulted books and visited dream interpreters, but I can find no answer." "Only God can interpret dreams," the Christian visitor told him, telling him that Jesus is the light of the world. "The light shining on you means that Jesus is calling you, and the stream may be an indication that you should be baptized." The Iranian was convinced and agreed to follow Jesus and be baptized.[3]

We have scores of similar testimonies of dreams and visions being used by God to draw individuals, families and entire communities to Himself. Similarly, the Lord uses this method of revelation in the lives of most, if not all, believers.

WHAT IS A DREAM?

A dream is a release of revelation (whether natural or spiritual) that comes at a time when your body is at peace and you are settled. Sometimes this is the only way God can communicate with you, because your soul is quiet enough for the Lord to speak deeply into your spirit. A dream is like a snapshot of something you can relate to in picture form. Ecclesiastes 5:3 speaks of a dream coming when there are many cares. It may be a subconscious response to the circumstances of your life or the Holy Spirit communicating to you. As Jane Hamon states in her book *Dreams and Visions*:

> Dreams are formed in the subconscious mind of a man or woman based on images and symbols which are unique to the individual, depending on his or her background, experience and current life circumstances. Dreams can communicate to us truth about ourselves— or others—which our conscious mind may have failed to acknowledge.
>
> Dreams can originate strictly within the natural mind or can be given as messages from God's Spirit and received within the mind of man. . . . If we compare the

communication of the Spirit of the Lord through dreams to other methods of divine communication mentioned in Scripture—prophecy, a word of knowledge, etc.—the primary difference is that dreams are given first to our subconscious minds before being perceived by our conscious minds.[4]

In the ancient eastern world, dreams were treated as reality. Dreams were considered to be the world of the divine or the demonic, and they often revealed the future. Dreams could be filled with revelation that would cause the dreamer to make the right decision for his or her future.

Israel was forbidden to use many of the same type of divining practices as Egypt and other neighboring countries and peoples. However, God would visit them in the night to communicate His will and way to them. This continued throughout the Bible. In the first two chapters of the New Testament alone, God gave direction through prophetic dreams five times.

We as Christians can receive revelation from dreams that are inspired by the Holy Spirit as well. For instance, I once had a dream when I was in prayer for a trip to Israel. My good friend and colleague Bobbye Byerly and I were going to be leading prayer for a meeting facilitated by Peter Wagner that would reconcile Arab Christian leaders and Messianic leaders. Quite a bit of warfare surrounded this meeting. I became very troubled while praying and called Bobbye to tell her that we should pray and fast for three days before going. Bobbye was having the same burden and agreed immediately.

On the second day of the fast, I fell asleep and dreamed that Barbara Wentroble, a well-known prophet, asked me, "So, you are going to Israel. There are two ways. Which way are you taking?" I told her the way we were going. In the dream it was as if I showed her a map and we wandered through the Arab desert to get to Israel. She then said, "You may go that way, but if you do, you will experience much warfare. There is a better way for you to take." I said, "Oh, what is that way?" She replied, "Go straight to Israel and meet with the leadership you know. Then, have your meeting with everyone else." I woke up and knew that God had revealed to me the direction Peter Wagner should take as he proceeded in pulling together this meeting. I encouraged him to first have a meeting with the leaders of Israel whom we knew. Then we could have the overall meeting and reconciliation time. This proved to be direct revelation from God and had a significant impact on the overall outcome of our mission.

WHAT IS A VISION?

The easiest way to describe a vision is to imagine you are having a dream, but you are awake. To those experiencing a vision, it often seems as if they have entered into a different reality, since they are seeing images of items and events with their spiritual eyes that are not physically there. Others in the room may not see what is going on because the person having the vision perceives a spiritual event.

Sometimes differentiating between vision and dream is difficult to determine, if not impossible. For instance, the circumstances in which the revelatory visions came to the seers of the Bible vary. They came in waking hours (see Dan. 10:7; Acts 9:7), by day (see Acts 10:3) and by night (see Gen. 46:2). But the visions had close connections with the dream state (see Num. 12:6; Job 4:13).

In the Old Testament, the recipients of revelatory visions were the prophets, "writing" (see Isa. 1; Obad. 1; Nah. 1) and "non-writing" (see 2 Sam. 7:17; 1 Kings 22:17-19; 2 Chron. 9:29), the outstanding examples being Ezekiel and Daniel. Some would write their visions. Other prophets would have other individuals record their visions. Habakkuk 2:1-4 (*KJV*) says, "I will stand upon my watch, and set me upon the tower, and will watch to see what He will say unto me, and what I shall answer when I am reproved. And the LORD answered me, and said, Write the vision, and make it plain upon tables, that he may run that readeth it. For the vision is yet for an appointed time, but at the end it shall speak, and not lie: though it tarry, wait for it; because it will surely come, it will not tarry. . . . the just shall live by his faith." Many times, prophets need to write their visions so that anyone going by can understand what God is saying and the direction He is giving. In the New Testament, Luke manifests the greatest interest in visions, reporting the visions of Zechariah (see Luke 1:22), Ananias (see Acts 9:10), Cornelius (see 10:3), Peter (see 10:10) and Paul (see 18:9). We find Paul treating visions with much reserve (see 2 Cor. 12:1). The book of Revelation is the ultimate vision.

In *The Future War of the Church*, Rebecca and I share an in-depth vision that the Lord gave me on December 31, 1985. Even though I dream often, I have only had five visions that were significant enough for me to record. This detailed vision gave direction for the changes in the Church of the future. It also warned of militant Islam and lawless acts coming against the Church. You can read the details of this in chapter 1 of *The Future War of the Church*.[5]

My pastor is Robert Heidler. His wife, Linda, is a wonderful, prophetic prayer leader and minister. She had the following vision:

In March of 1997, we were in a Sunday morning church service. I began to have a vision. In this vision, I knew that the Lord was coming to visit my house. I had cleaned everything cleaner than ever before. My carpets were cleaned, my curtains were washed and ironed, and everything was dusted and polished. I had fresh flowers on the table. I could not think of anything else to do to make my house ready for the Lord to come. It was the best it could possibly be.

All at once, the Lord was standing in my house. He had not come to the door; He just appeared. I did not know what to say or to do. He looked around and then pointed to one wall of my living room and said, "That whole wall has to go." I was in shock. That wall was the one between my living room and garage. My washer and dryer were on the other side of that wall. I wanted to protest, but as the Lord spoke the words, the wall shattered. Sheet rock, two-by-fours and wires protruded from the wall, and the room was covered in plaster dust.

Before I could recover from that, the Lord pointed to a room off the back of my house. In reality, I did not have a room like this, only in the vision. This room had all kinds of awards, pictures, trophies, medals and so on. It also had family heirlooms. The Lord pointed to that room and said, "That whole room has to go." Immediately, I thought of getting all my treasures out, but the Lord said, "And don't try to get anything out either." As I looked, a huge crane appeared in my back-yard and a wrecking ball swung across and demolished the room.

My house was a wreck, I was in shock and I didn't know what to do. This was not what I had anticipated, but it was very clear what the Lord knew needed to happen in my house.

I love this vision. It speaks for itself. The Lord is saying, "Even though you've got everything in order, get ready for the changes I am bringing!"

WHAT IS A NIGHT VISION?

The Scriptures refer to night visions several times. A night vision occurs when we are not sure if we are asleep or awake, and it tends to be right to the point.

In Acts 16:9-10 we read:

> And a vision appeared to Paul in the night. A man of Macedonia stood and pleaded with him, saying, "Come over to Macedonia and help us." Now after he had seen the vision, immediately we sought to go to Macedonia, concluding that the Lord had called us to preach the gospel to them.

Ira Milligan offers this insight:

> There is a difference between a dream and a night vision. A night vision requires little or no interpretation. In addition to the actual vision seen, a night vision usually has a voice speaking that gives the primary meaning of the vision. In contrast, a dream seldom lends itself to self-interpretation.[6]

DISCERNMENT IS KEY!

Whether we are talking about dreams, visions or night visions, we need to recognize that not all revelation communicated through these means is necessarily inspired by God. There are three different categories of dreams and visions, each of which can be traced to different sources:

1. Spiritual dreams and vision, which are inspired by God's Spirit

2. Natural, or soulful dreams and visions, which are produced by the natural processes of a person's mind, will and emotions

3. False or occultic dreams and visions[7]

It is important for us to exercise discernment in determining the source of dreams and visions. If not, we may base our life decisions on soulful desires, or the enemy may gain a ready inroad to thwart us in our destiny. Adapted from Jane Hamon's book *Dreams and Visions*, the following is a list of questions to ask ourselves as we determine what is behind a dream or vision:

1. **Is the message of the dream or vision consistent with the teachings, character and nature of Jesus?** All revelation from spiritual dreams and visions will lead us into a closer, more committed relationship with God.

2. **Does the message of the dream or vision lead to righteousness?** If the message of the dream is more self-serving or speaks to soulful desires, it may not be a spiritual dream.

3. **Is the message of the dream or vision consistent with doctrine, teaching and principles from the Word of God?** All spiritual dreams or visions will support and emphasize biblical truths.

4. **Do you feel a stirring of your spirit or emotions upon awaking?** In the book of Daniel, we see that the king had a greatly disturbing dream. When you feel impacted by a dream, it could be an indication that God is speaking to you.

5. **Does the dream or vision cause you to search your soul? Have pressing questions been answered within the context of the dream?**

6. **Is the dream recurring or similar to others you've had?** While this alone is not an indicator of a spiritual dream, in the context of the other questions posed here, it could offer a clue that the Lord is trying to get your attention repeatedly.[8]

ALWAYS TALK TO GOD ABOUT YOUR DREAMS

If, after reading these questions and applying your God-given discernment, you determine that your dream is more of a natural or soulful origin, or more demonic in nature, do not be discouraged. No matter what the origin of the dream, you can and should always talk to the Lord about what you have dreamed. You should not ignore what a dream may reveal about your emotions, and you can always ask God to clarify puzzling or disturbing dreams so He can bring His comfort and healing to your mind, will and emotions. If you discern that a dream is demonic in nature, it might be an indication of how the enemy is working to thwart your destiny, or it could be a call to a new level of spiritual warfare. All dreams have some level of significance in your life, and it is important to invite the Lord into the process of determining what each dream's level of significance may be.

LEAN NOT ON YOUR OWN UNDERSTANDING

Many of us have been in very difficult places. There was a particular time in my wife, Pam's, and my own life where we had almost insurmountable issues surrounding us. One night, Pam had a dream. In the dream, she was on a path that led through a wooded area, yet she could still see the sun. As long as she kept her eyes on the sun, she continued moving forward. Even though the light got brighter and brighter, when she got close to the end of the path, a huge boulder extended itself out from the forest, completely blocking the path. During the dream, she began to think, *How can I get past this? I must get out to the other side.* She then heard a voice say, "Don't try and go around this blockade. Don't try and go over it. Don't try and go through it. Speak to it and tell it to move." When she got up that morning, she said, "We are going to speak to the issues that are coming against us." We began to speak to each one, making prophetic declaration to it, and we watched changes begin to take place.

Proverbs 3:5-6 says, "Trust in the LORD with all your heart, and lean not on your own understanding; in all your ways acknowledge Him, and He shall direct your paths." Seek God. Listen carefully. Let Him speak to you. Lean not on your own understanding, but let Him give you the way through your circumstance.

Now let's take an in-depth look at interpreting dreams and visions.

Notes

1. Ira Milligan, *Understanding the Dreams You Dream* (Shippensburg, PA: Treasure House, 1997), p. 3.
2. Fiona Starr and Jonny Zucker, *Dream Themes: A Guide to Understanding Your Dreams* (China: Barnes and Noble Books, 2001), p. 10.
3. "Praying Around the World," *The Prayer Track News,* vol. 8, no. 2 (April/June 1999), p. 8.
4. Jane Hamon, *Dreams and Visions* (Ventura, CA: Regal Books, 2000), pp. 22-24.
5. Chuck D. Pierce and Rebecca Wagner Sytsema, *The Future War of the Church* (Ventura, CA: Renew Books, 2001), pp. 28-35.
6. Milligan, *Understanding the Dreams You Dream,* pp. 9-10.
7. Hamon, *Dreams and Visions,* p. 37.
8. Ibid., pp. 60-63.

CHAPTER SIX

INTERPRETING DREAMS AND VISIONS

For God may speak in one way, or in another, yet man does not perceive it. In a dream, in a vision of the night, when deep sleep falls upon men, while slumbering on their beds, then He opens the ears of men, and seals their instruction.

JOB 33:14-16

Whether or not we are aware of it, God often reveals instructions to us through dreams. We may not even remember the dream, but often we will awaken with a new sense of clarity because God has spoken to us in the night. Because God often seals our instructions through dreams, we need to know how to properly interpret them.

In the Bible, prophecy and dreams were to be tested in the same way. and according to Numbers 12:6, we find that prophecy and dreams were treated equally. Saul complained that God would not speak to him or answer him "by dreams or by Urim or by the prophets" (1 Sam. 28:6). By this we can infer that these were normal ways that people heard from God. We find three types of dreams in the Bible:

1. **A simple message dream.** In Matthew 1–2, Joseph understood the dreams concerning Mary and Herod. There was no real need for interpretation. These dreams were direct, to the point and self-interpreted.

2. **The simple symbolic dream.** Dreams can be filled with symbols. Oftentimes the symbolism is clear enough that the dreamer and others can understand it without any complicated interpretation. For instance, when Joseph had his dream in Genesis 37, he fully understood it, as did his brothers, to the point that they wanted to kill him, even though it had symbols of the sun, moon and stars.

3. **The complex symbolic dream.** This type of dream needs interpretative skill from someone who has unusual ability in the gift of interpretation or from someone who knows how to seek God to find revelation. We find this type of dream in the life of Joseph, when he interprets Pharaoh's dream. In Daniel 2 and 4,

we find good examples of this type of dream. In Daniel 8, we find a dream for which Daniel actually sought divine interpretation.

It is our job as ambassadors for Christ to be carriers and interpreters of God's revelation in this age.

Understanding symbols is important not only to interpret our own dreams, but also to give some direction to those who come to us. As we mentioned in the last chapter, God speaks to unbelievers through dreams. I would prophetically say that this is only going to increase in the days ahead, and God will need believers who know how to discern and interpret in order to lead many to Christ. It is our job as ambassadors for Christ to be carriers and interpreters of God's revelation in this age.

DANIEL'S MODEL OF INTERPRETATION

As we think about the process of dream and vision interpretation, the book of Daniel provides us with a good pattern to follow. The following is the story of King Nebuchadnezzar's dreams and the process through which Daniel interpreted them:

1. Daniel determined the source of the dreams and knew they were a message from God. This is the first step, which we discussed in chapter 5.

2. Daniel asked for time to interpret the dream (see 2:16). First Corinthians 2:6 says, "We do, however, speak a message of wisdom among the mature, but not the wisdom of this

age or of the rulers of this age, who are coming to nothing"
(*NIV*). In other words, we have wisdom that no one else has
access to—wisdom that comes from the Lord. We often need
time to seek the Lord for His interpretation, as well as wisdom
from those God has placed in our lives.

**3. Daniel gathered intercession by urging his friends to
seek the Lord (see 2:18).** At times, we need to soak the dream or
vision in prayer and ask those around us to intercede on our
behalf until clear interpretation of the vision comes from God.

4. Daniel gained revelation from the Lord (see 2:19). As
we pursue an interpretation, we can ask certain questions that
are helpful in gaining revelation over the dream or vision. These
include:

- To whom does the dream refer?
- What is it really about?
- What is the setting(s)?
- What is the symbolism in the dream? (There will be
  more about this later in the chapter.)
- What are the current circumstances and history of
  the one who received the dream or vision?
- What is God's timing in fulfilling the dream or
  vision? (Ask this question once there is a handle on
  the interpretation.)
- Based on this dream, what responsibility does the
  one who received the dream or vision have?

5. Daniel worshiped God (see 2:20-23). It is so important
to give God glory and to worship Him for both the dream or
vision and the interpretation. When we miss this, we miss the
next step of revelation in our lives.

6. Daniel explained the dream (see 2:36-45). When we
interpret a dream for someone else, we need to be sensitive as to

how the Lord would have us explain the interpretation.

MODERN-DAY DREAMS AND INTERPRETATIONS

When I was coming into the things of the Lord and the Spirit, the Lord placed a wonderful mentor in my life. Lacelia Henderson was a teacher in the public school system and a wonderful Bible teacher as well. Most importantly, she understood the spiritual realm in which I was just learning to maneuver. I want to encourage each of you reading this book to find someone who can help you as you move into receiving supernatural revelation. Lacelia had a dream that really has stuck with me through the years.

> In the dream, I had gone with friends (Charles and Charlene) to a cabin they had in the woods. We were dressed for bed when someone knocked at the door. Charlene started to answer the door, and I waited in the bedroom. I said I would hide back there while she answered the door. If it was a friend, I would come out, and if not, I would jump out the window and run for help. When she opened the door, these men came in who were dressed in army fatigues. They came in like the gestapo and took the place by storm (captured it). In the meantime, I had jumped out of the window in my nightgown. When they saw the open window, they knew that I had escaped. Some of them ran outside and got in a vehicle (like a jeep) to look for me. It was very, very dark; I was alone and vulnerable (in my nightgown). Their eyes pierced the night as they scanned to and fro trying to spot me. When they were not looking my way, I ran from tree to tree. It was all very intense, and I had very little time to

get behind the next tree before they looked back my way. Finally, I came to a clearing and saw some houses. I knew I had to choose the house to run to very carefully. It had to be someone who knew me and trusted me. I knew that once I stepped out into the clearing I would be spotted. I also knew that when I ran to a house to use the telephone to call for help I would not have time to explain the situation to get permission to use the telephone. If I took time to explain I would be caught and stopped by the enemy. Once I got to the house, I had to be able to run straight to the phone to make the call for help.

When I asked Lacelia to write this dream down, she commented to me, "After all these years (it's been 15 years so far), I can still remember every detail of this dream vividly." This dream was a warning! Not only did it warn of the need to know your relationships in the future, it explained that Christians would go into a new dimension of persecution. This was a dream that activated discernment and wisdom. A Scripture reference very appropriate for this dream is 1 Samuel 18:14-15: "And David behaved wisely in all his ways, and the LORD was with him. Therefore, when Saul saw he behaved very wisely, he was afraid of him." First Samuel 20:3 says, "But truly, as the LORD lives and as your soul lives, there is but a step between me and death." This dream revealed a changing government status, and from a spiritual standpoint showed that the "Saul government" of the Church would persecute those who were moving into a new wineskin.

In *The Future War of the Church*, Rebecca and I shared this when we listed the guidelines that will assist us in maintaining our spiritual focus and knowing the times we live in:

We must know how to get in touch with each other immediately. Maintaining our connections and relationships with each other is another key to securing our future. God sovereignly connects and aligns us with one another, so we can function effectively. Know with whom God has connected you and how to let them know what God is saying to you. This will keep God's warning system in proper order. One way that we remain connected is through frequent gatherings. In Genesis 49, we read that Jacob called his sons together and revealed their futures to them. The Lord is using prophetic gatherings today in much the same way. As we come together corporately, God will speak to us and reveal things we may not see on an individual basis. Another method God is raising up to maintain connections is through organizations like the World Prayer Center in Colorado Springs. The World Prayer Center uses state-of-the-art communications technology to both gather and disseminate information to praying people throughout the world on urgent matters that require immediate, fervent prayer. This is one way God is connecting the Body of Christ in order to secure the future harvest.[1]

Kristine Herman, who works for Wagner Leadership Institute, had the following dream:

In my dream, I was seated in a large room with tables, and people were eating and fellowshipping. I was seated and a man in a short-sleeved white sweater came up to me and told me that he thought the Lord wanted him to give me some money, so he gave me some cash. He ended up coming back several times and giving me more money. I didn't look to see how much he had given me. I got up from my chair and was walking away, looking in my wallet to see how much money he had given me. I found two 100-dollar bills along with some smaller bills totaling $250 to $300. I also found a blank check that he had signed. His name (Larry) and his wife's name were at the upper left corner of the check. I also had a credit card form with his credit card information on it and Larry, too, signed this.

Kristine interpreted this dream immediately:

My understanding while I was looking at the check and the credit card form was that I could purchase whatever I desired and there was no limit to the amount I could spend. I could pay off my mortgage with his personal check and that would be just fine.

I think God would give a dream like this to someone who is in a difficult place financially, or perhaps they are moving forward into an expanded vision and need to know that God is going to provide for them.

INTERPRETING SYMBOLISM

In most dreams recorded in the Bible, God used a tremendous amount of symbolism to convey His message. Jesus often used parables when making His points. This has not changed through the years. The vast majority of dreams and visions are laden with symbolic imagery. It is often helpful, therefore, to have a basic understanding of symbolism and to have reference books on hand with helpful, biblically based lists of symbols and types.[2] (See the appendix for a list of basic symbols.)

Snails and Turtles

I once had a dream about a friend in McAllen, Texas. In the dream, my friend was walking along a path filled with snails. If he did not stomp on the snails, they would turn into snakes that hissed and bit. There were also many turtles, and if my friend kept in line with the turtles, they would lead him safely to his destination.

As God showed me the interpretation, I realized the snails represented my friend's business associates who were linked with legal entities that had the ability to turn and bite. Through the turtles, God was saying that my friend needed to slow things down in order to prosper. As I shared this with my friend, he was amazed. At that time, he was involved in three separate lawsuits, and there were many "snails" in his life. The dream gave him wisdom as to how to proceed with these associates. Also, because he heeded the warning of the turtles and slowed things down, he did prosper and was ultimately successful in all his lawsuits and business ventures.

Symbols Are Flexible

Ira Milligan adds the following thoughts on interpreting symbols:

> Almost all symbols can have both positive (good) and negative (bad) meanings. . . . The most important thing to remember about interpreting symbols is, *never be narrow-minded.* Symbols, like words, are very flexible. When one knows the context of a dream and the circumstances of the dreamer's life, one can properly assign the right meanings. Without this knowledge one can only guess.
>
> For instance, it is possible for an ant in a dream to mean several different things . . . [these include] industrious; wise; diligent; prepared for the future; nuisance; stinging or angry words. When one dreams of ants at a picnic, the context would obviously lean

toward "nuisance" as the meaning of the symbol, even though it is their industrious nature that makes them such a nuisance! To dream of ants gathering food would relate directly to the key word definition of industrious, diligent preparation for the future. Likewise, dreaming of being bit or stung by ants would fit the "stinging or angry words" definition.

Sometimes a symbol has a meaning to one person that would not fit another. . . . When trying to decipher a symbol, the first question we should ask is, "What does this symbol mean to [the dreamer]?"[3]

A Complex Dream

In the spring of 1996, Linda Heidler had this dream while I was in Israel.

In the dream, I was with a large group of people out in a desert place. There was a lot of sand blowing, which would get into your eyes. I remember that my hair kept blowing into my face. We were all watching a woman who was seated at a large machine. She was sitting on a high stool behind the machine. The machine had lots of levers, pulleys, gears, buttons, pedals and so on. One by one the people from the crowd would stand in front of the machine and the woman would begin to talk to them. As she talked to them, she would start working the pedals and pulling the levers. She was moving constantly as she spoke to them. She would tell them things they needed to let go of and things they needed to increase in. As she spoke and worked the machine, the people all turned into triangles. When she was finished, she would put the people into clear plastic containers like Tupperware and seal them. When she had finished with two people, she would put them together and they would form a Star of David, then they would go off together as happy as could be.

As we watched, we would look at the person she was working on and say, "There is no way she can make them into a triangle." But one after another they would all form into triangles. Then when we saw who she was going to pair up to form the Star of David we would say, "There is no way those two will ever match up." But when she finished, they were perfectly matched and very happy.

When it was my turn to stand in front of the machine and she began to talk to me and operate the machine, it was just wonderful! Everything she said made so much sense. It was so wise and freeing and practical. I loved it! When she finished, I was a triangle. She then put me in the Tupperware and sealed me. I could not feel anything different, but I noticed that the sand was not blowing in my eyes anymore and my hair was not blowing in my face. I do not remember who I was matched up with to form the Star of David, but I felt complete.

This is a great example of a complex symbolic dream. First, it had relevance in Linda's life. Second, it applied to my trip in Israel. (See chapter 5 for my explanation of this dream of Israel that Barbara Wentroble was in.) And third, it had a great relevance concerning covenant alignment. To fully interpret the dream, I used Scripture as well as an understanding of symbols. I used several Scriptures to help in the interpretation of this dream along with the word of wisdom:

1. **Workmanship.** "For we are His workmanship, created in Christ Jesus for good works, which God prepared beforehand that we should walk in them" (Eph. 2:10).

2. **Sealed.** "Who also has sealed us and given us the Spirit in our hearts as a guarantee" (2 Cor. 1:22). "And do not grieve the Holy Spirit of God, by whom you were sealed for the day of redemption" (Eph. 4:30).

3. **Joined.** "Now I plead with you, brethren, by the name of our Lord Jesus Christ, that you all speak the same thing, and that there be no divisions among you, but that you be perfectly joined together in the same mind and in the same judgment" (1 Cor. 1:10). "But he who is joined to the Lord is one spirit with Him" (1 Cor. 6:17). "From whom the whole body, joined and knit together by what every joint supplies, according to the effective working by which every part does its share, causes growth of the body for the edifying of itself in love" (Eph. 4:16).

4. **Transformed.** "I beseech you therefore, brethren, by the mercies of God, that you present your bodies a living sacrifice, holy, acceptable to God, which is your reasonable service. And do not be conformed to this world, but be transformed by the renewing of your mind, that you may prove what is that good and acceptable and perfect will of God" (Rom. 12:1-2).

It would take quite a bit of space to write the full interpretation of this dream. But I think when you read the dream along with these Scriptures, you will find application to your life as well.

SYMBOLIC LANGUAGE

When we sleep, we are set aside from the contact of the culture and world around us. Therefore, if we dream, we sometimes can seem less civilized than our surroundings, but we also can seem wiser in our dreams than when we are awake. A world of pictures, images and silence exists that we really do not perceive in fullness many times when we are awake.

In his book, *Dreams*, Rabbi Shmuel Boteach states:

> Symbolic language is a language in which inner experiences, feelings, and thoughts are expressed as if they were sensory experiences or events in the real world. It is a language which has a different logic from the one we use while awake. By this logic, it is not time and space which are the ruling categories, as they are in the real world. Rather, symbolic language is governed by categories of intensity and association. It is a language with its own grammar and syntax, as it were, and a language one must understand if one is to comprehend the meaning of Midrashim, myths, and dreams. Symbolic language is the one universal language the human race has constantly developed. Yet it has been forgotten by modern man. Although he may still write his dreams with it, he is at a loss to decipher it when he awakens.[4]

REPLACING SYMBOLS WITH KEY WORDS

Once we have an idea of what the symbols represent, we can follow Daniel's example of interpreting the king's dream. He simply replaced the symbols with the key words or patterns that they represented in order to decipher the message in the dream. Referring again to the dream I had of my friend in McAllen, Texas, the simple interpretation would be that he was moving along in business (represented by the path) and that certain business associates surrounding him (represented by the snails) would turn and bite him (represented by the snakes) if he did not deal with them appropriately (represented by the stomping). Then the dream shifted to reveal that he would have to get in step with God's timing, which was slower than he was going (represented by following in line with the turtles) in order to prosper (represented by the safe destination).

When interpreting symbols for others, it is important to remember that we should not impose our interpretation of symbols if it does not bear witness with the dreamer.

Your Sons and Your Daughters Shall Prophesy . . .

My children have many dreams. Most of them have a real prophetic bent to them. They have been taught to listen carefully for the voice of God in their dreams. Pam and I try to let them share their dreams, good or bad, and then discuss various spiritual insights with them. Daniel, one of our older sons, had a dream a few years ago of watching the Chinese army muster to invade our nation. We had many discussions about this. Our daughter, Rebekah, had the following dream when she was 16:

My friend Randi and I were driving in the Expedition (our family vehicle). Randi was actually driving, and I was in the front passenger seat. I looked out the window and saw debris all around us. We were in a suburban area that had been blown up. I was probably in my early 20s (three or four years older than when I had the dream). I saw children playing in the debris. I also saw a family with a father and three boys. The boys were likely 17, 13 and 10 years old. They all looked alike. The four of them were holding hands as they walked through the debris. As they walked up to the car, Randi introduced me. The father recognized me and said, "It's nice to meet you. My wife used to be a big fan of yours." I was perplexed at why he used the past tense in referring to his wife. I next shook hands with the oldest son and felt like I knew him. Then we said we'd see them at the Love Feast at the church and drove off.

When we arrived at the church, the church itself was completely intact, but everything around it was blown up. I saw my friend, Micah, in the welcome center. As I walked over to see him, I passed the area where brochures were displayed. Underneath the announcement center at the church was a family photograph. It had matting and three photos of the same family that I had just seen on the drive to church. In the first picture, they were happy and content. There was a woman in the picture who was smiling. The second picture was just of the father and boys. They looked very different. The third picture was just of oldest son. In the photo, it appeared as if he had his hands pushing away the camera. I did not understand why this picture was included. As I visited with another friend at church, I kept thinking that I needed to help my friend Heather, but I didn't know where she was. I seemed to get distracted in conversation, but my overriding thought was that I needed to help Heather.

At this point, the whole dream repeated itself a second time. The dream then repeated itself a third time; however, this time, the atmosphere had changed for the worse. At the church, I went into the nursery to help Heather, but the nursery was completely destroyed. In this portion of the dream, I was 10 years older, and I was a doctor. I turned to a lady and told her that her child would be fine. Heather was at the opposite door in the nursery. She had a baby who I knew would be fine. Upon leaving the nursery, I was much younger again. Things had not been destroyed and looked as they presently are today. I met someone in the hall who shared they were happy for me. I noticed Mom was in the church entrance. I overheard her say there was a new family coming to the church whose mother was really sick. At this point, that family entered the building and I realized it was the family at the beginning of my dream. The mother had cancer and was dying. When I saw and shook the oldest boy's hand, I asked him if we met before. He said, "No." Then the dream ended.

This is a very interesting dream with great spiritual significance. The dream is a three-tiered dream, which reveals three stages of Rebekah's life and three stages of the family's life. The dream also reveals three stages of destruction resulting in future restoration, and three stages of the Church in days ahead. Notice that the dream repeated itself three times. Generally, if a dream is repeated, it becomes a very sure and necessary revelation for the future. I could take this dream and prophesy tremendously to us, saying, "Fear not the devastation ahead, for God has a restorative plan. He will be bringing in many who are sick and afflicted. He will be restoring families. If we will follow Him and feast with Him, we will always be successful in the destiny of our lives."

HOW DO WE PREPARE TO RECEIVE DREAMS FROM GOD?

Chances are that whether or not you are aware of it, you have received messages from God in your dreams. Now that you have a bit more understanding, the following is a list of practical things you can do to prepare yourself for future occurrences:

1. Keep an open mind. Don't be frightened about receiving God-inspired dreams.

2. Make sure your bedroom is in peace and conducive to hearing the Spirit of God. If you have ungodly objects, such as gargoyle statues or Ouija Boards in your bedroom (or anywhere in your home for that matter), the Spirit of God will not be able to flow as freely because you have an open door to demonic activity. Do all you can to invite the Holy Spirit into your bedroom.[5]

3. Ask what your sleep habits are like. Do you have sleep deprivation? Is your sleep frequently interrupted? Often the enemy will attempt to keep you from being refreshed so that it will be difficult to perceive what God is saying. Try to get your sleep patterns in good order so your sleep is refreshing and rejuvenating.

4. Pray before you go to sleep and ask the Lord to speak to you, and expect to receive spiritual dreams.

5. Have a pen and notebook near your bed to write down impressions. If it is easier, keep a tape recorder nearby. Record every detail you can remember. If you can remember it, there may be a good reason why. Record the setting, progression, symbols, colors, people—everything you can remember. Also, if your dream changes scenes, continue to record it as one dream because, even though it may have different scenes, it is probably all one message. It is also a good idea to keep a dream diary so you have a record to refer to in days ahead. Often the Lord will use a series of dreams to convey a message. It is possible to miss the full impact of what God is saying without this kind of record.

6. Ask the Lord to help you remember your dreams. Dreams are fleeting. Job 20:8 says, "He will fly away like a dream, and not be found; yes, he will be chased away like a vision of the night." There is often a short span of time in which you can clearly recall your dreams. Also, we have not trained ourselves to remember dreams because few of us understand their true significance. Of course, there will be times when we still cannot remember our dreams, but the Lord can help us with our recall.

7. Give yourself time when you awaken to record your dreams and meditate before the Lord. Because you generally have a short window of time upon awakening to record dreams when they are more vivid, I recommend giving yourself about a half hour between the time you awaken and the time you get out of bed in which to meditate on what the Lord may have been speaking to you in the night. This is a good time to ask God to begin giving you an interpretation of your dream.

8. Be sure you respond to the revelation God gives you through your dreams in the same way you would to a prophetic word or to other Holy Spirit-inspired revelation in your life. As we have stated throughout this book, all revelation from God requires a response from you.

Notes

1. Chuck D. Pierce and Rebecca Wagner Sytsema, *The Future War of the Church* (Ventura, CA: Renew Books, 2001), pp. 22-23.
2. Some excellent resources for interpreting symbols include Ira Milligan, *Understanding the Dreams You Dream* (Shippensburg, PA: Treasure House, 1997) and *Every Dreamer's Handbook* (Shippensburg, PA: Treasure House, 2000); Jane Hamon, *Dreams and Visions* (Ventura, CA: Regal Books, 2000); Kevin J. Conner, *Interpreting the Symbols and Types* (Portland, OR: City Christian Publishing, 1999); and Ed F. Vallowe, *Biblical Mathematics: Keys to Scripture Numerics* (Columbia, SC: Olive Press, 1995).
3. Ira Milligan, *Understanding the Dreams You Dream*, pp. 31-33.
4. Rabbi Shmuel Boteach, *Dreams* (Brooklyn, NY: Bash Publications, 1991), p. 17.
5. For further insight into spiritual housecleaning, we highly recommend Chuck D. Pierce and Rebecca Wagner Sytsema, *Protecting Your Home from Spiritual Darkness* (Ventura, CA: Regal Books, 2004).

CHAPTER SEVEN

GOD IS READY TO PERFORM HIS WORD!

You will be a joy to all generations, for I will make you so. . . . You will know at last that I, the Lord, am your Savior and Redeemer, the Mighty One of Israel. . . . Salvation will surround you like city walls, and praise will be on the lips of all who enter there. . . . All your people will be righteous. . . . The tiniest group will become a mighty nation. I, the LORD, will bring it all to pass at the right time.

I S A I A H   6 0 : 1 5 - 2 2 ,   *N L T*

When we hear God's voice, we should allow our expectations in Him to arise! In our book *The Best Is Yet Ahead*, Rebecca and I explain that "future" and "expectation" are synonymous. Our future is linked with an expectation of God moving. This is a time for the Church to have its expectation level renewed and raised to another level. Isaiah 59 and 60 are wonderful prayer guides to see this happen in our lives. Hope must transcend and move into faith. Faith then produces overcoming, and overcoming leads to a demonstration of God's power and a manifestation of His promises:

> Therefore prophesy and say to them, "Thus says the Lord GOD: 'Behold, O My people, I will open your graves and cause you to come up from your graves, and bring you into the land of Israel. Then you shall know that I am the LORD, when I have opened your graves, O My people, and brought you up from your graves. I will put My Spirit in you, and you shall live, and I will place you in your own land. Then you shall know that I, the LORD, have spoken it and performed it,' says the LORD" (Ezek. 37:12-14).

Notice that the phrase "I will place you in your own land" was the prophetic fulfillment released in Ezekiel 36, where the Lord said, "But you, O mountains of Israel, you shall shoot forth your branches and yield your fruit to My people Israel, for they are about to come" (Ezek. 36:8). The word of the Lord had come full circle! As we explained in chapter 2, four levels of agreement and prophesying were necessary for Ezekiel to see the fulfillment of God's word. What if Ezekiel had stopped pressing forward after the bones came together, but there was no breath in them? That's what we tend to do in the Body of Christ. We think we've heard God prophesy, but when things don't turn out as we thought, we too often give up and end up falling short of reaching our prophetic destiny. We do not see the word that God has spoken to us coming to fulfillment. As Ezekiel prophesied through to the end, resurrection power was released so that the graves opened and the people were set in their own land.

I love this phrase, "'Then you shall know that I, the LORD, have spoken it and performed it,' says the LORD" (Ezek. 37:14). It's one thing for there to be a promise in our lives that we know is from God, but it's another thing for that promise to be performed in our lives. We cannot be a people that faint easily. Discouragement has no place in us as God's people. If we choose not to back up or stop, but to keep moving forward through the levels of prophecy, God will perform His will in us and bring about prophetic fulfillment!

In Jeremiah 1, we see God calling and commissioning Jeremiah to go forth to bring restoration through change and warning. Verses 11 and 12 summarize what I feel the Lord is saying as we enter the next season ahead:

> Moreover, the word of the LORD came to me, saying, "Jeremiah, what do you see?" And I said, "I see a branch of an almond tree." Then the LORD said to me, "You have seen well, for I am ready to perform My word."

Perhaps these verses will enable us to pray and trust the Lord to enter into the fullness of His plans concerning our lives.

HE CAUSES EYES TO OPEN!

The phrase "What do you see?" appears throughout the Bible in places where the Lord asks this question of His people. In Luke chapter 2, when Jesus Christ was born of Mary and the glory of the Lord manifested in the earth, the shepherds out in the fields, keeping watch over their flocks by night, were startled and even fearful of this manifestation. The angel of the Lord came to them and said not to be afraid, for great joy had entered the earth realm. He actually said, "Rejoice, for the unlocking redemptive force for your life has now come to the earth" (paraphrased).

Suddenly, all the heavenly hosts began to praise. Once this host departed, the shepherds talked among themselves and said, "Let us now go to Bethlehem and see this thing that has come to pass, which the Lord has made known to us." And when they had seen Him, they told everyone what the angels had said to them (see Luke 2:8-17).

In days ahead, there will be times of manifestation of the Lord's glory. Do not fear this manifestation. Be willing to open your eyes to what the angelic hosts are doing around you. See your provision manifest! See your joy restored! See change come into your sphere of authority! Once you *see*, be willing to declare what the Lord is doing!

HE IS THE BRANCH

"I see a branch of an almond tree," Jeremiah replied to the Lord. The branch was a symbol of kingship and prosperity (see Dan. 11:7; Job 8:16). The Lord is described as *the* "Branch," both righteous and beautiful (Isa. 4:2; Jer. 23:5; Zech. 3:8; 6:12). *The* Branch produces branches, and we are branches of the true Vine (see John 15:5-6).

Branches of trees (palm, myrtle, willow and others) were used ceremonially at the Feast of the Tabernacles for making booths (see Neh. 8:15). This symbolically shows us that eventually we, as His branches, will overlay each other to form a covering of safety as we participate in His glory in the earth. Those who understand the Branch will rule.

Back to Jeremiah's response to the Lord—he specifically saw an almond tree. The almond was significant in that it was the first tree to bloom. It also was used as a breeding device to increase Jacob's herds (see Gen. 30:38). It was one of the best fruits of the land that was given as a gift (see Gen. 43:11). Aaron's rod produced ripe almonds signifying the priesthood to

As the Lord speaks to you, you need to wake up and watch for things to intensify in your life. Watch for a new blossoming!

come (see Num. 17:8). The early appearing white bloom of the almond was linked to the graying head that signifies wisdom. Jeremiah was called to watch, and when he saw the almond, it meant that spring was coming. The almond symbolized "wakeful hastening." As the Lord speaks to you, you need to wake up and watch for things to intensify in your life. Watch for a new blossoming! Do not fear pruning, for the Branch has come for you to "branch out" and be fruitful. Declare this over your life.

HE COMES TO AFFIRM HIS GLORY

The promises of God are "yea and amen." Once we see what God would have us see, He begins to put a "yes" down deep within us. The affirmation of God also is linked with favor. The favor of God upon us causes us to experience pleasure, desire and delight. He delights in us when we see His path for us and move accordingly.

Favor also is linked with a manifestation of God's glory. God's glory (Hebrew, *chabod*) means His weightiness. We experience God's glory when we see His honor, splendor, power, wealth, authority, magnificence, dignity, richness, fame and excellence. Knowing His will and experiencing His glory breaks us out of naïveté, instability, vanity and the thought processes that assume everything is temporary. Once we experience this affirmation of God's will and glory, we will hear God saying to us, "For with God, nothing will be impossible." The affirmation of God causes His Glory to be seen.

HE WAS AND IS OUR "I AM"

"I AM" was God's response to Moses' request in Exodus 3:13-14. This means, "I AM who I AM"; "I will be who I will be"; or even "I cause to be that which is." God's response is not a name that limits God in any way. Rather, it is an affirmation that God is always free to be and act as He wills.

Jesus' I AM responses in several New Testament passages suggest more than the simple identifying "I am He." The I AM of Mark 6:50 means, "I AM Jesus and not a ghost." It suggests the divine I AM who alone "treads on the waves of the sea" (Job 9:8; see Mark 6:48-49) and makes the waves hush (see Ps. 107:28-29; compare Mark 4:39). John 8:24 helps us see that Jesus as the I AM is a matter of eternal life and death for us: "For if you do not believe that I am He, you will die in your sins."

Many of us never recognize what His true identity of I AM means to us:

- I AM is **Jehovah** (*Jeh hoh' vuh*). Declare Him as "LORD."
- I AM is **Jehovah-Jireh** (*Jeh hoh' vuh-ji rehh*). Declare,

"Yahweh will provide" (see Gen. 22:14). It is the name Abraham gave to the place where the Lord provided a sacrifice in place of Isaac. He made Abraham "see" his provision.

• I AM is **Jehovah-Rapha** (*Jeh hoh' vuh-ray' fuh*). Declare, "He has healed." In Exodus 15, He is the One who healed the children of Israel so they could move forward toward the promise. He really was saying, "You need a healer. I AM He who heals."

• I AM is **Jehovah-Nissi** (*Jeh hoh' vuh-nihs' si*). Declare, "Yahweh is my banner." Moses declared Jehovah as banner and built an altar to Him after defeating the Amalekites (see Exod. 17:15). This name is linked with deliverance and miracles.

• I AM is **Jehovah-Shalom** (*Jeh hoh' vuh-shah luhm*). Declare, "Yahweh is peace." Gideon built an altar to the God of peace (see Judg. 6:24). I AM is the One who can make you whole. Once Gideon understood this part of His character, he was released to go to war against his enemies. I AM is the strategy to defeat your enemies.

• I AM is **Jehovah-Shamma** (*Jeh hoh' vuh-shuhm' maw*). Declare Him as "The Lord is there." The Jerusalem of Ezekiel's vision was known by this name. Compare Isaiah 60:19-20 and Revelation 21:3. May you sense, feel and know His presence.

• I AM is **Jehovah-Tsidkenu** (*Jeh hoh' vuh-tsihd kee' new*). Declare Him as "The Lord [is] our righteousness" (Jer. 23:6; 33:16). The name is applied to a future Davidic king who would lead his people to do what is right, thus bringing peace (23:6) and restoring the city of Jerusalem (33:16). You are the righteousness of God in Christ Jesus!

KNOW I AM AS THE PRINCE OF PEACE

Peace is a state of rest, quietness and calmness. Peace is an absence of strife leading to tranquility. Peace denotes wholeness—body, soul and spirit—and perfect well-being. Peace includes harmonious relationships between God and humans, between one another, and between nations and families. Jesus, the Prince of Peace, gives peace to those who call upon Him for personal salvation.

Luke 1:79-80 says He came "'to give light to those who sit in darkness and the shadow of death, to guide our feet into the way of peace.' So the child grew and became strong in spirit." I believe this is the will of the Prince of Peace in our lives. Matthew 10:34 says, "Do not think I came to bring peace on earth. I did not come to bring peace but a sword." These two statements seem contrary. However, what the Lord is saying is, "Let me cut away every earthly tie that distracts you from *My* best will in heaven for your life. I long to see you whole and filled with peace. So let Me cut away that which will keep you from being whole and experiencing My covenant blessings."

GOD IS READY TO PERFORM HIS WORD!

When God is ready to move, it means He is watching, waking, hastening and anticipating the perfect time to align with His saints in the earth and release His will to be manifested in our midst. To be ready means that He is sleepless, alert, vigilant and on the lookout to cause the supernatural door in heaven to open and pour out His will in the earth. To be ready means He is watchfully looking for the opportunity to care for us in a new way. To be ready means He is watching to begin to build and plant in the earth that which He has blueprinted in heaven.

When God was ready to move to give His Son to you as a gift, He began to order and orchestrate events for that release. He does the same thing in your life. Watch for the ordered events. Be assured that He is watching over you. Watch with Him so that when He opens doors for you, you enter into a new dimension of freedom, victory and glory.

Once you abide in Him, He can accomplish, confirm and continue His will in your life in order to bring you into His full plan. He can cause you to endure your circumstances and enemies so that they do not stop you from advancing into the ultimate victory He has for your life.

To perform means to stir up, strengthen, succeed, accomplish, advance and appoint. To perform means He will release industrious ability within us, so that as we journey on the path He has given us and sacrifice before Him, we will feel His presence and power. To perform also means to assemble, fight, muster together and wait upon the war ahead. In waiting, He comes to our aid to demonstrate His love and ability in our lives. When He performs, He fulfills, finishes, gathers, governs and grants to us that which we need to complete our assignments victoriously.

Blessed is she [or we] that believed: for there shall be a performance of those things which were told her [or us] from the Lord (Luke 1:45, *KJV*).

He was sent "to perform the mercy promised to our fathers and to remember His holy covenant" (Luke 1:72).

And being fully convinced that what He had promised He was also able to perform (Rom. 4:21).

Being confident of this very thing, that he which hath begun a good work in you will perform it until the day of Jesus Christ (Phil. 1:6, *KJV*).

There will be a performance! Let Him be the performance of your life. Lay down your own performance and enter into His!

IN CLOSING

We hope this book has helped you recognize when God is speaking and also to embrace the voice of God in your life. May the Lord richly bless you as you seek to hear His voice and obey His will for your life! We are praying for you to hear the voice of God in a new way.

DREAM SYMBOL INTERPRETATION

As you will notice, many of the following symbols have conflicting interpretations assigned to them, some positive and some negative. This list is only meant to be a general guide. The symbol always needs to be interpreted in light of the context of the dream or vision, in light of what the symbol means to the dreamer and by the guidance of the Holy Spirit.[1]

NUMBERS

One. Unity, God, beginning, first, rank, order, new
Two. Division, judge, separate, discern, agreement, witness; union (two becoming one)

Three. The Trinity, deity, conform, obey, copy, imitate, likeness, tradition, completeness, perfect, testimony; connected with the bodily resurrection of Christ and His people

Four. The earth (four winds, four corners), reign, rule, kingdom, creation; unsaved or fleshly man; boundaries

Five. Grace, redemption, atonement, life, the Cross, government (five-fold gifts), works, service, bondage (including debt, sickness, phobias and so on), taxes, prison, sin, motion

Six. Humanity, the beast, Satan, flesh, carnal, idol; manifestation of sin

Seven. Complete, all, finished, rest, perfection

Eight. Put off (as in putting off the old self), sanctification, manifest, reveal, new beginnings, resurrection, die, death; new order of things

Nine. Manifestation of the Holy Spirit, harvest, fruitfulness, fruition, fruit of the womb, finality, fullness; perfection or divine completeness

Ten. Judgment, try or trial, test, temptation, law, order, government, restoration, responsibility, tithe; Antichrist kingdom; testimony

Eleven. Mercy, end, finish, last stop, incompleteness, disorganization, disintegration, lawlessness, disorder, the Antichrist; judgment

Twelve. Joined, united, govern, government, oversight, apostolic fullness, the holy city of God; governmental perfection

Thirteen. Rebellion, backsliding, apostasy, revolution, rejection, double blessing, double cursing; depravity

Fourteen. Passover, double, recreate, reproduce, disciple, servant, bond slave, employee; deliverance or salvation

Fifteen. Free, grace, liberty, sin covered, honor; rest

Sixteen. Free-spirited, without boundaries, without law, without sin, salvation; love

Seventeen. Spiritual order, incomplete, immature, undeveloped, childish; victory

Eighteen. Put on (as in the Spirit of Christ), judgment, destruction, captivity, overcome; bondage

Nineteen. Barren, ashamed, repentant, selflessness, without self-righteousness; faith

Twenty. Holy, tried and approved, tried and found wanting; redemption

Twenty-one. Exceeding sinfulness, of sin

Twenty-two. Light

Twenty-three. Death

Twenty-four. Priestly courses, governmental perfection

Twenty-five. The forgiveness of sins

Twenty-six. The gospel of Christ

Twenty-seven. Preaching of the gospel

Twenty-eight. Eternal life

Twenty-nine. Departure

Thirty. Consecration, maturity for ministry

Thirty-two. Covenant

Thirty-three. Promise

Thirty-four. Naming of a son

Thirty-five. Hope

Thirty-six. Enemy

Thirty-seven. The Word of God

Thirty-eight. Slavery

Thirty-nine. Disease

Forty. Probation, testing, ending in victory or defeat; trials

Forty-two. Israel's oppression, the Lord's advent to the earth

Forty-five. Preservation

Fifty. Pentecost, liberty, freedom, jubilee; Holy Spirit

Sixty. Pride

Sixty-six. Idol worship

Seventy. Prior to increase, multitude; universality, Israel and her restoration

Seventy-five. Separation, cleansing, purification

One hundred. Fullness, full measure, full recompense, full reward; God's election of grace, children of promise

One hundred nineteen. The resurrection day; Lord's day

One hundred twenty. End of all flesh, beginning of life in the Spirit; divine period of probation

One hundred forty-four. God's ultimate creation and redemption; the Spirit-guided life

One hundred fifty-three. God's elect, revival, ingathering, harvest; fruit bearing

Two hundred. Insufficiency

Six hundred. Warfare

Six-Six-Six. Antichrist, Satan, mark of the damned, mark of the man who is a beast; the number of the beast

Eight-Eight-Eight. The first resurrection saints

One thousand. Maturity, full stature, mature service, mature judgment; divine completeness and the glory of God

COLORS

Amber. The glory of God

Black. Lack, sin, ignorance, grief, mourning, gloomy, evil, ominous, famine, burned, death

Blue. Spiritual, divine revelation, visitation, authority, Holy Spirit, depressed (as in feeling blue), male infant, hope; medium or dark blue can be God's Spirit or Word, blessing, healing, goodwill; very light blue can be spirit of man, evil spirit, corrupt

Brown. Dead (as in plant life), repentant, born again, without spirit

Crimson. Blood atonement, sacrifice, death

Gray. Unclear, vague, not specific, hazy, deception, hidden, crafty, false doctrine; gray hair can be wisdom, age or weakness

Green. Life, mortal, flesh, carnal, envy, inexperienced, immature renewal; evergreen can be eternal life or immortal

Orange. Danger, great jeopardy, harm; a common color combination is orange and black, which usually signifies great evil or danger; bright or fire orange can be power, force, energy

Pink. Flesh, sensual, immoral, moral (as in a heart of flesh); chaste, a female infant

Purple. Royal, kingship, rule (good or evil), majestic, noble

Red. Passion, emotion, anger, hatred, lust, sin, enthusiasm, zeal, war, bloodshed, death

White. Pure, without mixture, light, righteousness, holiness of God, Christ, the angels or saints, blameless, innocence

Yellow. Gift, marriage, family, honor, deceitful gift, timidity, fear, cowardliness

CREATURES

Alligator. Ancient, evil out of the past (through inherited or personal sin), danger, destruction, evil spirit

Ant. Industrious, wise, diligent, prepared for the future, nuisance, stinging, angry words

Ass (donkey). Lowliness, patience, strength, endurance, service

Ass (wild mule). Untamed human nature, stubborn, self-willed, unsubdued, depraved, obnoxious, unbelief

Bat. Witchcraft, unstable, flighty, fear

Bear. Destroyer, evil curse (through inheritance or personal sin, including financial loss or hardship), economic loss, danger, opposition, evil, cunning, cruel, strong, ferocious

Beaver. Industrious, busy, diligent, clever, ingenious

Bees. Produce sweetness, power to sting, host of people, affliction, busybody, gossip

Bird. Spirit, Holy Spirit, demon, man, gossip, message; (see crow, dove, eagle, owl, vulture)

Bull. Persecution, spiritual warfare, opposition, accusation, slander, threat, economic increase

Butterfly. Freedom, flighty, fragile, temporary glory

Calf. Increase, prosperity, idolatry, false worship, stubbornness, prayers, praise, thanksgiving, enlargement (e.g., when a calf breaks out of a stall)

Camel. Burden-bearer, servant, endurance, long journey, ungraceful

Cat. Self-willed, untrainable, predator, unclean spirit, bewitching charm, stealthy, sneaky, crafty, deception, self-pity, something precious in the context of a personal pet

Chicken. Fear, cowardliness; hen can be protection, gossip, motherhood; rooster can be boasting, bragging, proud; chick can be defenseless, innocent

Crow (raven). Confusion, outspoken, operating in envy or strife, hateful, direct path, unclean, God's minister of justice or provision

Deer. Graceful, swift, sure-footed, agile, timid

Dog. Strife, contention, offense, unclean spirit, unbelievers; pet dog can be something precious, friend, loyal; dog wagging tail can be friend, acceptance; dog biting can be rewarding evil for good, betrayal, unthankful; barking dog can be warning, incessant nuisance, annoyance; dog trailing game can be persistent, obsession; rabid dog can be single-minded pursuit of evil, contagious evil, persecution, great danger; bulldog can be unyielding, stubborn; watchdog can be watchman, elder, minister (good or bad), alert, beware

Dove. Holy Spirit, gentleness, sacrifice

Dragon. Satan, evil spirits, Antichrist forces

Eagle. Leader, prophet (true or false), minister, fierce predator, sorcerer, strength, swift

Elephant. Invincible or thick-skinned, not easily offended, powerful, large

Fish. Souls of humanity (both clean and unclean), character, motive

Fox. Subtlety, deception, cunning, false prophet, wicked leader, hidden sin, sly and evil people

Frog. Demon, witchcraft, curse, evil words, puffed up, unclean

Goat. Sinner, unbelief, stubborn, argumentative, negative person, accuser, Satan

Hawk. Predator, sorcerer, evil spirit, warrior, unclean

Horse. Strength, swiftness, power, spiritual support, power of the flesh, spiritual warfare, age

Lion. Dominion, Christ, king, regal, bold, power, Satan, religious tradition, courage, royalty

Mice. Devourer, curse, plague, timid

Monkey. Foolishness, clinging, mischief, dishonesty, addiction

Moth. Deterioration, destructive, deceitful, undetected trouble, corruption

Owl. Circumspect, wisdom, demon, curse, night bird

Pig. Ignorance, hypocrisy, religious unbelievers, unclean people, selfish, gluttonous, vicious, vengeful

Rabbit. Increase, fast growth, multiplication; hare can be Satan and his evil spirits

Raccoon. Mischief, night raider, rascal, thief, bandit, deceitful

Rat. Unclean, wicked person, jerk, devourer, plague, betrayer

Roach. Infestation, unclean spirits, hidden sin

Scorpion. Sin nature, lust of the flesh, temptation, deception, accusation, destruction, danger, a whip

Serpent (snake). Curse, demon, deception, threat, danger, hatred, slander, witchcraft, wisdom

Sheep. Chant, the people of God, innocent

Spider. Evil, sin, deception, false doctrine, temptation; spiderweb can be snares, lies

Tiger. Danger, powerful minister (both good and evil)

Vulture. Scavenger, unclean, impure, evil person or spirit, all-seeing, waiting for evil opportunity

Wolf. Predator, devourer, false prophet, personal gain, wicked and false teachers, destroyer of God's flock

OTHER

Acid. Bitter, offense, carrying a grudge, hatred, sarcasm

Apples. Fruit, words, sin, temptation, appreciation, fruit of the Spirit

Arm. Strength or weakness, savior, deliverer, helper, aid, reaching out, striker

Ashes. Memories, repentance, ruin, destruction

Automobile. Life, person, ministry

Autumn. End, completion, change, repentance

Baby. New beginning, new idea, dependent, helpless, innocent, sin

Bed. Rest, salvation, meditation, intimacy, peace, covenant (marriage, natural or evil), self-made

Bicycle. Works, works of the flesh, legalism, self-righteousness, working out life's difficulties, messenger

Blood. Life of the flesh, covenant, murder, defiled, unclean, pollution, purging, testimony, witness, guilt

Boat. Support, life, person, recreation, spare time, personal ministry

Brass. Word of God or man, judgment, hypocrisy, self-justification, fake, human tradition

Brother-in-law. Partiality or adversary, fellow minister, problem relationship, partner, oneself, natural brother-in-law

Clouds. Change or covering, trouble, distress, threatening, troubling thoughts, confusion, hidden

Dancing. Worship, idolatry, prophesying, joy, romance, seduction, lewdness

Diamond. Hard, hardheaded, hard-hearted, unchangeable, eternal, gift of the Spirit, something valuable or precious

Door. Entrance, Christ, opportunity, way, avenue, mouth

Dreaming. A message within a message, aspiration, vision

Drowning. Overcome, self-pity, depression, grief, sorrow, temptation, excessive debt

Drugs. Influence, spell, sorcery, witchcraft, control, legalism, medicine, healing

Earthquake. Upheaval, change by crisis, repentance, trial; God's judgment, disaster, trauma, shock

Eating. Partake, participate, experience, outworking, covenant, agreement, friendship, fellowship, devour, consume

Elevator. Changing position, going into the spirit realm, elevated, demoted

Eyes. Desire, covetousness, passion, lust, revelation, understanding

Falling. Unsupported, loss of support (financial, moral, public), trial, succumb, backsliding

Father. Authority, God, author, originator, source, inheritance, tradition, custom, Satan, natural father

Father-in-law. Law, authoritative relationship based on law, legalism, problem authoritative relationship, natural father-in-law

Feet. Heart, walk, way, thoughts (meditation), offense, stubborn (unmovable), rebellion (kicking), sin

Finger. Feeling, sensitivity, discernment, conviction, works, accusation (as in pointing a finger), instruction

Flowers. Glory, temporary, gifts, romance

Foreigner. Alien, not of God, of the flesh, demonic

Forest. Foreboding, fearful place, often associated with confusion or without direction

Friend. Self; the character or circumstance of one's friend reveals something about oneself; sometimes one friend represents another (look for the same name, initials, hair color); sometimes represents actual friend

Gold. Glory or wisdom, truth, something precious, righteousness, glory of God, self-glorification

Grandchild. Heir, oneself, inherited blessing or iniquity, one's spiritual legacy, actual grandchild

Grandparent. Past, spiritual inheritance (good or evil), actual grandparent

Grapes. Fruit, spirit of promise, fruit of the Spirit, promise of wrath

Hair. Covering, covenant, humanity, doctrine, tradition, old sinful nature

Hands. Works, deeds (good or evil), labor, service, idolatry, spiritual warfare

Iron. Strength, powerful, invincible, stronghold, stubborn

Kiss. Agreement, covenant, enticement, betrayal, covenant breaker, deception, seduction, friend

Knees. Submission, obey, worship, service, stubborn, unyielding

Lead. Weight, wickedness, sin, burden, judgment, fool, foolishness

Mechanic. Minister, Christ, prophet, pastor, counselor

Mirror. God's Word or one's heart, looking at oneself, looking back, memory, past, vanity

Miscarriage. Abort, failure, loss, repentance, unjust judgment

Money. Power, provision, wealth, natural talents and skills, spiritual riches, power, authority, trust in human strength, covetousness

Mother. Source, Church, love, kindness, spiritual or natural mother

Mother-in-law. Legalism, meddler, trouble, natural mother-in-law

Nudity. Uncovered or flesh, self-justification, self-righteousness, impure, ashamed, stubborn, temptation, lust, sexual control, exhibitionism, truth, honest, nature

Oil. Anointing; clear oil can be the Holy Spirit anointing, healing; dirty oil can be unclean spirits, hate, lust, seduction, deception, slick, danger of slipping

Pen/pencil. Tongue, indelible words, covenant, agreement, contract, vow, publish, record, permanent, unforgettable, gossip

Pregnancy. In process, sin or righteousness in process, desire, anticipation, expectancy

Pumpkin. Witchcraft, deception, snare, witch, trick

Rain. Life, revival, Holy Spirit, Word of God, depression, trial, disappointment

Silver. Knowledge of God (redemption), knowledge of the world (idolatry)

Sister. Spiritual sister, Church, self, natural sister

Spring. New beginning, revival, fresh start, renewal, regeneration, salvation, refreshing

Stone. Witness, word, testimony, person, precept, accusations, persecution

Storm. Disturbance, change, spiritual warfare, judgment, sudden calamity or destruction, trial, persecution, opposition, witchcraft

Summer. Harvest, opportunity, trial, heat of affliction

Table. Communion, agreement, covenant, conference, provision; under the table, can be deceitful dealings, hidden motives, evil intent

Tin. Dross, waste, worthless, cheap, purification

Train. Continuous, unceasing work, connected, fast, Church

Tree. Person or covering, leader, shelter, false worship, evil influence; oak can be strong shelter; willow can be sorrow; evergreen can be eternal life

Tunnel. Passage, transition, way of escape, troubling experience, trial, hope

Van. Family (natural or Church), family ministry, fellowship

Water. Spirit, Word of God, the spirit of man or the spirit of the enemy, unstable

Wind. Spirit or doctrine, Holy Spirit, demonic or strong opposition, idle words

Window. Revealed, truth, prophecy, revelation, understanding, avenue of blessing, exposed, an unguarded opening for a thief to enter

Wine (strong drink). Intoxicant, strong emotion (such as joy, anger, hate, sorrow); Spirit of God or spirit of man, revelation, truth, witchcraft, delusion, mocker

Winter. Barren, death, dormant, waiting, cold, unfriendly

Wood. Life, temporary, flesh, humanity, carnal reasoning, lust, eternal, spiritual building material

Wrestling. Striving, deliverance, resistance, persistence, trial, tribulation, spirit attempting to gain control

Note

This list of dream symbol interpretations is compiled from the following references: Kevin J. Conner, *Interpreting the Symbols and Types* (Bible Temple Publishing, 1992); Jane Hamon, *Dreams and Visions* (Regal Books, 2000); Ira Milligan, *Understanding the Dreams You Dream* (Treasure House, 1997); Ed F. Vallowe, *Keys to Scripture Numerics* (Ed F. Vallowe Evangelistic Association, 1966). For further explanation or biblical references on any of the listed symbols, or for complete lists, please see these references.

RECOMMENDED READING

Bickle, Mike. *Growing in the Prophetic*. Lake Mary, FL: Charisma House, 1996.

Cooke, Graham. *Developing Your Prophetic Gifting*. Grand Rapids, MI: Chosen Books, 2003.

Conner, Kevin J. *Interpreting the Symbols and Types*. Portland, OR: City Christian Publishing, 1999.

Deere, Jack. *Surprised by the Voice of God*. Grand Rapids, MI: Zondervan Publishing Company, 1996.

Hamon, Bill. *Prophets and Personal Prophecy*. Shippensburg, PA: Destiny Image Publishers, 1987.

Hamon, Jane. *Dreams and Visions*. Ventura, CA: Regal Books, 2000.

Jacobs, Cindy. *The Voice of God*. Ventura, CA: Regal Books, 1995.

Joyner, Rick. *The Prophetic Ministry*. Wilkesboro, NC: MorningStar Publications, 2003.

Lord, Peter. *Hearing God*. Grand Rapids, MI: Baker Books, 1988.

Milligan, Ira. *Every Dreamer's Handbook: A Simple Guide to Understanding Your Dreams*. Shippensburg, PA: Treasure House, 2000.

Milligan, Ira. *Understanding the Dreams You Dream*. Shippensburg, PA: Treasure House, 1997.

Vallowe, Ed F. *Biblical Mathematics: Keys to Scripture Numerics.* Columbia, SC: Olive Press, 1995.

Yocum, Bruce. *Prophecy.* Ann Arbor, MI: Servant Publications, 1976.

SUBJECT INDEX

SCRIPTURE INDEX